# THE CRISIS OF BAD PREACHING

"Rev. Joshua Whitfield believes that the cure for the crisis of preaching in the Catholic Church is not for the preacher to learn a few practical skills. Good preaching flows from the being of the preacher and so it is impossible without a deep life of prayer and study. He pulls no punches. This book offers just the challenge that we need to hear. It is beautifully written and filled with wisdom."

**Timothy Radcliffe, O.P.**
Former Master of the Order of Preachers

"How can we ever hope to reach the lost if we continue to deliver homilies that don't engage and inspire? Joshua Whitfield urgently calls on preachers, and all those who work with them and hear them, to reexamine the importance we place on our Catholic preaching. His historical perspective is illuminating and his insight into taking control of one's message will resonate with anyone who has ever felt a homily wasn't working as it should. He reminds us of the privilege we have in preaching the Gospel, and that when done well, it will prepare our people to receive Jesus. This book will convince you that the New Evangelization starts in *your* pulpit."

**Rev. Michael White and Tom Corcoran**
Authors of *Rebuilt*

"Steeped in the classics, while drawing on a breadth of modern Catholic and Protestant greats, Whitfield invites homilists to take seriously their vocation to preach—avoiding the 'delusion of inspiration' and embracing the hard work of preparing preaching that comes from the heart and speaks to the heart. He reminds homilists that theirs is not simply a craft but a discipline that touches every aspect of the preacher's life."

**Ann M. Garrido**
Associate Professor of Homiletics
Aquinas Institute of Theology

"Well done! Fr. Joshua Whitfield's book is reflective, encouraging, and to the point. He offers an inspirational challenge to those called to the ministry of preaching to do so with great resolve, passion, preparation, and conviction. Whitfield beckons the preacher 'to beg the Holy Spirit to set fire to us and our words. We must renew ourselves in the way we pray and prepare and deliver homilies.'"

**Rev. Anthony F. Lackland**
Vice Rector of Holy Trinity Seminary

"Priests and deacons, add this book to your library! Fr. Whitfield has given us a vital and important work for our time. He reminds all of us who preach how we can fulfill this calling with passion and power—and help renew not only our preaching but also our Church."

**Greg Kandra**
Blogger at *The Deacon's Bench*

"I hope bishops, priests, deacons, and seminarians read this book. I hope leaders of the Church heed the call of Joshua Whitfield and give our clergy the training and support they need to become better preachers. We lay Catholics ought to read this book too, so we can champion this cause. The Church desperately needs relevant, compelling, and inspiring preaching each and every Sunday. Fr. Joshua Whitfield is showing us a way to get there."

**Jim Moroney**
Publisher Emeritus
*Dallas Morning News*

"Joshua Whitfield writes that we live in a 'darkening age of shrinking faith.' Anyone who can turn such a phrase has something important to say. What Whitfield has to recommend for the renewal of preaching by Roman Catholics is at once simple and profound. Protestants, too, will find this work urgently compelling. With passion and humor, Whitfield reminds us that preaching and the preacher are inseparable. Hopefully his book will mark a new day for many who have the happy task of glorifying God through the proclamation of the Good News."

**Stanley Hauerwas**
Gilbert T. Rowe Professor Emeritus of Divinity and Law
Duke Divinity School

"I hope for the renewal of Roman Catholic preaching that Joshua Whitfield heralds in this book, for it will usher Christ's kingdom closer for the blessing of the world. I wish I'd written this book. But since God gave Fr. Joshua such gifts of wisdom, humor, and passion, I'll reread his book, teach it, recommend it, and will look forward to seeing God use it mightily."

**Rev. Jason Byassee**
Butler Chair in Homiletics and Biblical Hermeneutics
Vancouver School of Theology, University of British Columbia, Vancouver

"Joshua Whitfield's new book on the heart and way of the preacher fills a gaping hole in the formation of clergy. In his engaging style, he draws on the classics of rhetoric, the rich tradition of Protestant homiletics, and his own experience as preacher, husband, and dad. With a wealth of references, he helps preachers understand their task and urges them to continue their education. More importantly, Whitfield points out that a preacher must first *hear* the Word. He is calling not only for a reform of Catholic homiletics but also of the way we live our priesthood."

**Rev. Peter Verhalen, O.Cist.**
Abbot
Cistercian Abbey of Our Lady of Dallas

"Joshua Whitfield sends out an impassioned vision for all in the Church to embrace: 'preachers lit ablaze' and 'inspired listeners' are to walk hand in hand as missionary disciples. Whitfield urges homilists to preach from the heart, from the inside out, in a determined effort to set hearts ablaze with a desire for God. He pleads for all of us to listen for the Spirit in every homily, no matter how challenging that might be. To revitalize the Church, together we need to renew our preaching. In this fervent and fast-moving book, Whitfield implores us all to pray and work to do just that."

**Karla J. Bellinger**
Author of *Connecting Pulpit and Pew*
Associate Director of the John S. Marten Program for Homiletics and Liturgics
University of Notre Dame

# THE CRISIS OF BAD PREACHING

## Redeeming the Heart and Way of the Catholic Preacher

JOSHUA J. WHITFIELD

AVE MARIA PRESS AVE Notre Dame, Indiana

© 2019 by Joshua J. Whitfield

Founded in 1865, Ave Maria Press is a ministry of the United States Province of Holy Cross.

www.avemariapress.com

Paperback: ISBN-13 978-1-59471-835-9

E-book: ISBN-13 978-1-59471-836-6

Cover image © joyfnp/GettyImages.

Cover and text design by Samantha Watson.

Printed and bound in the United States of America.

*Library of Congress Cataloging-in-Publication Data is available.*

*To A. A. W.*

The world has not heard its best preaching yet.
—Phillips Brooks, *The Joy of Preaching*, 42

# CONTENTS

# PREFACE

He was a preacher . . . and never charged nothing for
his preaching, and it was worth it too.
—Mark Twain, *The Adventures of Huckleberry Finn*, 175

Let's be honest. A lot of preaching today is bad—some is even terrible.
Sunday by Sunday, preaching is often trite, self-involved, or simply dull.
My preaching, your preaching, our preaching, the preaching you hear
from the pews: so much of it falls short, so much unworthy of God
and unworthy of the mission. We should admit this. Candidly and in
penance, we should acknowledge the failures and the crisis that our
too-often lackluster preaching has brought to the Church. The matter
is urgent.

Pope Benedict XVI, forever circumspect but no less frank, said
once that "the quality of homilies needs to be improved" (*Sacramentum
Canitatis*, 46). Pope Francis, characteristically more blunt, said that we
preachers too often trap Jesus in our "dull categories," and that we all
"suffer because of homilies: the laity from having to listen to them and
the clergy from having to preach them!" (*Evangelii Gaudium*, 11, 135).
These sentiments, echoed the world over by people in the pews, bear
witness to the problem. In his introduction to *A Handbook for Catholic
Preaching*, Timothy Radcliffe, O.P., begins by asking, "Why are most
homilies so boring?" as if it's a truism needing no argument.[1] Google
"bad Catholic preaching" and you'll spend the next several hours reading blog posts and articles and comments, all of them offering the same
sad assessment. Preaching is not good, and the mission of the Church
is suffering because of it.

Of course, it's not just Catholic preaching. Protestant preaching isn't what it used to be either, not for some time. At the beginning of his multivolume work on Christian preaching, the Protestant preacher and scholar Hughes Oliphant Old writes, "Like so many other preachers of my generation, I find myself asking what has happened to preaching."[2] It's a decline felt in the pews too. Kendrick Lamar, for example, the popular rapper, made headlines recently talking about the "emptiness" of the sermons he heard as a child.[3] It's a decline that's been felt for years. More than a half century ago, Martin Luther King Jr. lamented that too often "the contemporary church is a weak ineffectual voice with an uncertain sound."[4] Having been corrupted by prosperity-Gospel delusions, twisted patriotism, or therapeutic idioms of tired progressivism, Protestant preaching is also in crisis. And for that, too, the mission of Jesus suffers.

Throughout the Church's history, preaching has at times suffered and at other times flourished. Beatrice in Dante's *Paradiso*, for example, criticizes the preachers of her time for "inventing new ideas." "Christ did not say to His first congregation: 'Go preach idle nonsense to the world,'" she complains.[5] Bad preaching is nothing new. Still, the poverty of preaching in our day is an urgent crisis, an evangelical crisis impossible to ignore.

Never mind that we live in an age of generally poor public speaking and impoverished orality, an age overwhelmed by miniscule, fragmented digital texts and shallow memes. It's an age, as Mark Thompson, CEO of the *New York Times*, wrote, witnessing the collapse of "public language" and the rise of a "rhetoric of rage."[6] More tragically, we preachers have contributed to it. The substance of many sermons or homilies is often no longer the substance of the Gospel, a sin of omission belonging to both conservatives and liberals, traditionalists and progressives. I often wonder about the providence that placed the Creed after the homily: Was God seeing to it that after a bad homily his people would hear at least some essential truth?

And again, it's a crisis because our bad preaching is part of the reason so many people have given up the practice of the faith or have left the Church. It's why some either have given up on Christ altogether or simply refuse to consider the Lord meaningfully at all. For an untold number of ordinary people, the Gospel no longer even dawns on them, not faintly. For them, Christianity or the Church or anything pertaining to faith simply isn't in the conversation. As Charles Taylor said, ours is truly a secular age, one in which materialist narratives enjoy "the false aura of the obvious."[7] That is, for a growing number of people, it just doesn't occur to them to look to the faith for any sort of wisdom at all, much less salvation. Today, social scientists, celebrities, economists, random doctors, and sham gurus all enjoy more default credibility than your average preacher. Johann Hari, for instance, is a best-selling author—brilliant, humane, and important. One of his books, *Lost Connections*, about the causes of depression and anxiety, runs almost three hundred pages long.[8] Almost every page details his discovery, via social scientists, of wisdom basic to Christianity and Judaism, ancient wisdom lived for centuries. But Hari doesn't see that. He dismisses faith in one parenthetical phrase. For him, he seeks wisdom everywhere but from the Church. And that's because the Church has probably never spoken meaningfully to him, her witness never compelling. And that's not Hari's fault. It's ours.

Which is why I say we preachers need to repent, rouse ourselves from clerical lethargy, and get to work becoming better preachers. Because the matter is urgent, and believe it or not, souls are at stake. And because there's still hope!

There remains great power in the human voice, power in language and rhetoric, not to mention the power of the Gospel. Even in this visual age of digital ephemera, it is still possible for the orator, as Socrates said long ago, to touch souls with words.[9] The homily, as a form of meaningful communication, still has immense potential.

There still is evangelical power and possibility in the homily as a Christian practice. It is still possible for a homily or sermon to speak to the needs of the faithful as well as bear witness to the wider world the truths of the Gospel. The homily can still accomplish something social media will never be able to, and that's because a homily shares more fully in the kerygma, the proclamation of the Gospel that is also God's voice, the voice of the Shepherd, which gives life (see Jn 5:25). That is, a homily can still change lives more powerfully than any meme.

I'm a parish priest, not a homiletic scholar. I'm a rhetorical amateur. But I do preach every day, as do so many of my fellow clergy. I live the craft day in and day out. And I'm also a convert. I grew up around good preaching. I grew up loving words, and I loved listening to well-crafted words and to the rhythms of the human voice. If there's anything good about my preaching today, I owe it mainly to the Protestant preachers who've influenced me since my youth. And as a convert and a priest, I believe that although the Catholic Church is rich in tradition, she is too often poor in practice. So much has been written and offered in the Church about preaching, a veritable treasure of wisdom and theology. Yet little has been the fruit.

Which is why I've written this book—a manifesto of sorts—again, not as an expert, but simply as a preacher. As preachers, we must rediscover our place as public intellectuals, as members of a great company of preachers across time and traditions, and as persons of the Church. And we must learn to beg the Holy Spirit to set fire to us and our words. We must renew ourselves in the way we pray and prepare and deliver homilies. Because, as I said, the matter is urgent.

Little of this book is original. More an act of personal *paradosis*, I simply offer what has formed me as a preacher, and how it's formed me. As the philosopher Michel de Certeau said, "In spite of a persistent fiction, we never write on a blank page, but always one that has already been written on."[10] Preachers rarely emerge wise solitaires from the desert, infused with wisdom by God himself. Most of us are the products of the Holy Spirit's human mediation, what I call in this book the communion of preachers. That's how I was formed, by the preachers in my life and by the rhetorical wisdom of collected centuries, which is a wisdom that still speaks and which we must hear if the renewal of our preaching is to have depth.

So—apologies upfront—I quote a lot of people. I'm an eclectic thinker, more just a reader. As Bl. John Henry Newman once said of Richard Whately, I think and often write "by the medium of other brains."[11] And that means I talk a lot about Aristotle and St. Augustine and others, and especially about Phillips Brooks, an old preacher whose 1877 Lyman Beecher Lectures on Preaching influenced me more than anything else as a preacher. If anything, if this book inspires some of my fellow preachers to read Phillips Brooks's lectures or Aristotle's *On Rhetoric* or Augustine or Fred Craddock, I'll consider myself successful. St. John Chrysostom may call me a thief for weaving into my own words the flowers of others, but that's fine with me.[12]

But another thing: This is a book about the renewal of *Roman Catholic* preaching, particularly the preaching of homilies within the context of the Mass. And, as everyone knows, such preaching in the Catholic Church is at present almost exclusively reserved for ordained clergy—that is, for men. This is, of course, subject to debates and arguments of a particularly institutional and culturally Catholic kind, and for which I have neither expertise nor voice. I simply must note that in writing this book, and reflecting upon my own formation as a preacher, I have sensed, and come to lament, the contemporary absence of the rich tradition of women preachers, a tradition replete with beautiful and powerful preaching and that I think the Church would do well to recover, celebrate, and hear. Writing this book, as may show in some of the clumsiness of my language, I have tried to leave readers space to experience the same absence I feel and to think about it. I make no appeal. I offer only my obedience. Nonetheless, I think this, too, belongs to the renewal of preaching.

This book was written with my fellow Catholic clergy in mind. First, it's a book offered in charity and humility to my father bishops and my brother priests and deacons. But it's also offered in charity and humility and hope to all my fellow preachers from all denominations and all confessions. We preach the same Christ. We labor in the same vineyard. My prayer is that we continue to preach in charity and ecumenical hope—until we are one, until the appearing of Christ. But I also offer this book to all my brothers and sisters in the common priesthood of Christ, the lay faithful. The epilogue is written primarily for you, but my hope is that you will listen in on the whole conversation, so that we may each do our part in the renewal of preaching, together as the Body of Christ. Because it will take all of us, not just those ordained to preach.

My hope is to rouse my fellow clergy as well as my brothers and sisters in the pews, to rouse us all to bring good preaching back to the Church. Because the homily is an act of worship, we owe it our best.[13] For the sake of the mission, it's imperative that we seek the renewal of preaching. For the sake of the Church and for the sake of souls, it's time to begin, yesterday.

"And how can they hear without someone to preach?" (Rom 10:14). It's a question that is still relevant. And it's a question that should frighten us, inspire us, and spur us on—each of us, but especially us preachers.

That is, if we're worthy of the pulpit.

# ACKNOWLEDGMENTS

Thanks to every Catholic I've ever met. When I came into the Church, worn out and tired, the hospitable grace I received from so many quite literally saved me, and my wife and children too. In the grace found in them, we found God's grace, charity of the purest kind.

Profound thanks to the people of St. Rita Catholic Community in Dallas, Texas, for their inexhaustible grace and openness. Their care marked for the better my family forever, and I simply cannot write words beautiful enough to thank them.

Thank you to my brother priests, especially in Dallas. Without hesitation, they accepted me, offering me the fellowship of a presbyterate heroic and joyful. These are priests I love and with whom I'm honored to serve. Again, words are inadequate.

But also for the bishops, my words fail. Cardinal Kevin Ferrell, Bishop Kevin Vann, Bishop Mark Seitz, Bishop Robert Coerver, Bishop Greg Kelly, and Bishop Edward Burns: these are my fathers in God, each of whom played their part in helping me find my way and who continue to inspire me. To each I will always be grateful for their evangelical and apostolic love. They are true successors of the apostles, and I feel their communion.

With deep gratitude to the Cistercians of Our Lady of Dallas. For years and for many people, they have been a community of genuine spiritual care. I can't fathom where I'd be without them, without Fr. Roch especially. For this book particularly, I'm grateful for the week of hospitality given me, without which this book would not have been completed.

I'm likewise grateful to Eileen Ponder and the good people of Ave Maria Press for believing in me and helping me in more ways than I can number. And to the remarkable, joyful, and profound Lisa Hendey for calling me one day out of the blue.

But also I'm grateful for so many who've shaped me along the way, for those great preachers and mentors since childhood who taught me about Jesus and who preached the Gospel and inspired me. They know who they are. *Ut unum sint.*

And finally, I am grateful to my wife, Alli, and my children: Magdalene, Peter, Zoe-Catherine, and Bernadette. To my kids, for the joy they give Daddy when he comes home tired, and to my wife, for her pure love and unconquerable strength. I'm grateful for all they are. To say the least, it's a unique and demanding vocation to be the wife of a Catholic priest as well as a mother of four; but Alli is simply beautiful and strong inside and out, and she does it all with a rare grace. For everything, for her love and friendship and for the love she has for God and for our children, I'm thankful. Because, as I said, it's beautiful, and because it's holy. Thank you.

# PART I:
# REDEEMING
# THE HEART OF
# THE PREACHER

But the things that come out of the mouth come from
the heart.
> —Matthew 15:18

It begins with the heart, that innermost part of us. Good preaching
begins there. Jesus pointed to the heart. Criticizing the elders and teachers of his day, he said it was the wickedness of the heart that was to
blame. What comes from the mouth comes from the heart, Jesus said,
"and they defile" (Mt 15:18). Evil thoughts, found first in the heart, next
are spoken—evil words instead of good. This was the problem, Jesus
said. It's why the Pharisees, scribes, elders, and others were so caught
up with externals, with rituals and rules—because it was a way to ignore
the heart.

He was speaking, of course, the spiritual language of Judaism, but
also of humanity. As the mysterious center of every person, the heart
holds the emotions, reason, and will. In the heart, a person stands clos-
est to God either in consolation or in judgment, before the God who

"knows the heart" (Acts 1:24; 15:8). The heart is the person, the inner beginning and end, the origin of either good or evil. It's what finally explains a person after all other explanations have been given.

So, if it was true for the Pharisees and scribes, it's also true for us, for preachers. As for them, so for us: "from the fullness of the heart the mouth speaks" (Lk 6:45). Preaching today, we are often silenced by externals. Not just by rituals and rules but also by administration, the latest parish or diocesan appeal, the latest gimmick or slogan, or even by our own clunky, worn-out methods of preaching, we get lost and lose the point. Caught up with the methods and machinery of modern ministry, we lose touch with the heart.

All of this causes the preacher to suffer, and preaching even more so. Hollow, hackneyed, impersonal, shallow, and trite, it becomes the sort of preaching too often heard today: disembodied voices quoting ecclesiastical tracts, verbiage full of church-speak, which few know and even fewer care to know. James Mallon said the first question people often ask is whether the preacher is real.[1] Often the answer is no. Often it's as if homilies are preached by those who've never lived, ignorant of a world outside the Church; they preach about their hobbies, vacations, and pets, never more personally invested in their preaching than that. Too many homilies today fail the first test of human speech, which, as Socrates said, is to move the soul.[2] And that's because we've not put our own souls into it; our hearts are kept safe as we speak in borrowed clichés to people who see right through us.

A crisis of the heart, we preachers today should allow ourselves to be scolded by the Lord, seeing ourselves in some respects the Pharisees of our age. I'm not talking about hypocrisy or anything like that but about the heart, how we've allowed our preaching to become so stale and silly that we're just not heard anymore.

As Yves Congar put it decades ago, our preaching often just isn't "real." Our homilies come across "prefabricated," as we speak too often "like licensed dealers of orthodox formulas that sound impersonal and fixed."[3] Hans Urs von Balthasar wrote of that fear sometimes found in priests, which hides behind misused authority—a fear of a genuine encounter with people, which is born from a "lack of love."[4] It's what digs a chasm between preacher and people, making the homily a waste of time no matter how long or brief. Worrying about the length of homilies, talking about short attention spans, has nothing to do with it. It's about fear and the lack of charity in the heart of the preacher, the inhumanity of speech.

What's lacking is what Pope Francis called "synthesis." When as preachers we merely relay ideas or "detached values," and at the same time fail to "share" ourselves in the dialogue of preaching, we lack "synthesis." Preaching comes across cold, distant, and inhuman. The heart, Francis said, lacking fire and enlightenment, fails to join the hearts of listeners to the heart of God, all because the preacher's heart isn't in it. (*Evangelii Gaudium*, 142–143).

This is what's primarily the matter. This is what's wrong. And this is where the renewal of Catholic preaching must begin: with the heart. Before we can say anything about the way of the preacher, we must say something about the heart, how it's shaped, and how it beats.

# Heart, Ethos, Personality

To speak in terms of classical rhetoric, I'm talking about what Isocrates called nature or, better, what Aristotle called *ethos* or character. Philosopher and lover of logic though he was, Aristotle understood that effective persuasion had as much to do with a speaker's character as with arguments, that it was *ethos* that made the speaker "worthy of credence."[5] Isocrates thought similarly that formal training helped those already endowed with a natural ability for speaking.[6] Both understood that a good speaker was not made by rhetorical training alone. Yet Aristotle's notion of character is richer, as it considers both human nature and the idea that human nature can be trained, educated, and habituated.[7]

Thus, it's helpful to think about preaching the way Aristotle thought about rhetoric—that is, in terms of *ethos*, *pathos*, and *logos* and also *lexis*, *taxis*, and *hypokrisis*—all of which we will explore later in this book. Thinking about the character of the speaker, we can then consider the character of our congregations, what we're going to say, and how to say it. What Aristotle called *pisteis*, the means of persuasion, involve careful consideration of all of this; and anything like real renewal in Catholic preaching should take account of it too. But it must begin with character, with what's innermost. Renewal must begin with the heart.

# From Within

The model, of course, is Jesus. He is the one who "reveals" the Father, doing what his Father does, speaking what his Father speaks (see Jn 1:18; 5:19; 8:28). And he is the one who sends us and who has given us his Spirit, even promising to inspire our speech (see Mk 13:11; Jn 20:21). But again, it all begins interiorly.

In John's gospel, there are words of Jesus at once textually ambiguous and theologically enlightening, which illustrate this point. In Jerusalem on the last day of the feast of Tabernacles, the great Jewish feast recalling the Hebrews' journey to the Promised Land as well as God's abundant provision in the wilderness, Jesus stood up and said, "Let anyone who thirsts come to me and drink" (Jn 7:37).

Jesus seemed to be likening himself to the provision Yahweh supplied his people in the desert. Like water from rock, now Jesus offers the water of his Spirit to those who believe. A few verses later, he called himself the "light of the world," again like the pillar of fire that guided the people through the desert (Jn 8:12). But the ambiguous yet enlightening part is what he said next: "Whoever believes in me, as scripture says: 'Rivers of living water will flow from within him'" (Jn 7:38).

Living water will flow from "within him." But who's "him"? Many read "him" to mean Jesus, while others read it to mean the believer, but the text isn't clear. Does living water flow "from within" Jesus or "from within" those who believe in Jesus? That's the textual ambiguity.[8]

But it's also what's theologically enlightening. Because it reveals at once the interiority and the mystical union with Christ that is demanded of the preacher. As Christ is like the rock and the pillar of fire in the desert, feeding and guiding believers, so too are the preachers of Christ. From within both flow the living water of the Spirit. For both Christ and his preachers, it all begins "from within," from the heart.

The renewal of preaching begins with the renewal of the heart, the renewal of the preacher's *ethos* or character. Preaching once to students in Paris, St. Bernard of Clairvaux began by saying, "Clearly, then, the conversion of souls is the working of the divine, not the human, voice." And he asked his listeners to "make an effort to hear God speaking within rather than man speaking without."[9] That's the final achievement of the preaching event: people hearing in our voices "God speaking within."

To say the renewal of preaching begins with the renewal of the heart isn't to say something sentimental and meaningless. To say it's a matter of *ethos* is to say it's a matter of education and habituation. It means that preachers must take up again, or for the first time, those formative habits that will make them better preachers, practices that cultivate the virtues of preaching and the character of the preacher.

It isn't magic. It takes work, work we preachers need no longer neglect. And that's the purpose of the first part of this book: to suggest what the redemption of the preacher's heart looks like in the contemporary Church.

It looks like this. Today the preacher must become a public intellectual, embracing unashamedly the intellectual responsibility that goes along with modern ministry. The homilist must also consciously belong to the communion of preachers, learning and speaking from within the broad company of all who've preached the Gospel. And the preacher must be unquestionably a person of the Church, obedient to the voice of Christ in the Church, rather than to one's own voice. Again, all of this is for the sake of what Jesus and great preachers such as Bernard spoke of: so that the water of the Spirit may flow from within, and so that the divine voice may speak through the human voice.

# Truth through Personality

Yet before anything else, right here at the start, let me share what I think is the most important lesson a preacher should learn. If unlearned, there is nothing any book or any class can offer, no tip or insight that will help. For me, it's the first practical truth of preaching.

The famous nineteenth-century Protestant preacher Phillips Brooks described it best. He defined preaching as "the bringing of truth through personality." For him, that's what separated preachers: either the absence or the presence of personality:

> Truth through Personality is our description of real preaching. The truth must come really through the person, not merely over his lips, not merely into his understanding and out through his pen. It must come through his character, his affections, his whole intellectual and moral being. It must come genuinely through him. I think that, granting equal intelligence and study, here is the great difference which we feel between two preachers of the Word. The Gospel has come *over* one of them and reaches us tinged and flavored with his superficial characteristics, belittled with his littleness. The Gospel has come *through* the other, and we receive it impressed and winged with all the earnestness and strength there is in him. In the first case, the man has been but a printing machine or a trumpet. In the other case, he has been a true man and a real messenger of God.[10]

This, really, is the heart of the matter, talking as we are about the heart of the preacher. To renew the heart of the homilist is to enliven it, so that what is offered may truly be *felt* by the people, the Gospel pulsing through the words and even the body of the preacher.

More than charisma, preaching from the heart with personality is about preaching in personal immediacy to the people, and even sometimes with personal vulnerability. That's what moves people, what draws them to the Gospel: truth through personality. It's what leads people to what Aristotle called *pathos*—that is, to the right emotion, enabling them to listen well.[11] It's what Phillips Brooks meant when he said, "Let a man be a true preacher, really uttering the truth through his own personality, and it is strange how men will gather to listen to him."[12]

Too much preaching, in tone and gesture, simply lacks personality. Whether due to fear, poor training, or inexperience, so much preaching today rings hollow. Clunky, formulaic, cut and pasted, impersonal, it just doesn't touch listeners. And that's because listeners have nothing to touch in return—no person, no heart, just a voice, just words.

What's missing is what Karla Bellinger called "connection." Today more than ever, what we need to recover is what she called the "homiletical human bond."[13] Fred Craddock called it "passion," preaching like it personally matters. "To preach as though nothing were at stake is an immense contradiction,"[14] he said. The preacher, in the preaching event, can be—and sometimes ought to be—the "center of meaning" in a homily. That is, in preaching, just as in many other forms of public speaking, personality is as persuasive as words. The preacher should be a "mediator of meaning"[15] in whom the people recognize not only the word of God but also themselves, which demands the preacher be recognizably human, but without offering homiletic "useless digressions which risk drawing greater attention to the preacher than to the heart of the Gospel message" (*Verbum Domini*, 59).

But often this is precisely what frightens us, and it's why we don't always resist the "temptation to be ineffective."[16] Often we don't want to preach that Gospel, the Gospel that comes from the heart, because it would mean we'd have to let it change *us*. The Gospel that we want to cut the hearts of our people, we don't want to let cut our own. Often we resist this sort of preaching because it would mean that we'd have to undergo conversion too, when all along we thought ordination would be enough.

If Catholic preaching is to be renewed, it must begin with the heart, *ethos*, personality, and passion of each preacher. George Whitfield, the great revivalist preacher, said, "We can preach the Gospel of Christ no further than we have experienced the power of it in our hearts."[17] True of evangelicals, it's true of Catholics as well. It's the heart that must be prepared to catch divine fire if that fire is to catch our people. To renew preaching, we must prepare ourselves for a new Pentecost and make ourselves kindling ready for the Spirit. But first, before fire, the heart.

# 1.

# THE PREACHER AS PUBLIC INTELLECTUAL

For a priest's lips preserve knowledge, and instruction is to be sought from his mouth, because he is the messenger of the LORD.

—Malachi 2:7

Every person has a right to an opinion, but not every opinion is valuable. That's just true, however harsh it sounds. And it's also true for preachers, however impious it seems.

Cicero taught that speaking well is a matter of eloquence and wisdom, that wisdom without eloquence is of little use and that eloquence without wisdom is dangerous.[1] And Augustine agreed, adding that it is wisdom that comes first.[2] Again, this is true for all public speaking, preachers included.

If the goal of rhetoric is to persuade, as both the pagan philosopher and Doctor of the Church agree—that is, if the function of rhetoric is to *teach* for the sake of understanding, to *delight* for the sake of enjoyment, and to *sway* for the sake of obedience—then the preacher needs to be, without embarrassment or folksy false humility, a student, a reader, and even a theologian.[3] The preacher must be unashamedly intellectual, however pretentious that sounds. For the heart of the preacher, for *ethos*, the mind matters. To put it bluntly, to preach well today, preachers

9

need to get smarter and to keep getting smarter. And they need to do the work it takes to get smarter, developing the habits of intelligence demanded by the times.

The wisdom required of the preacher does not issue automatically from the grace of ordination, like some magical gift inherent in the Sacrament of Holy Orders. There is, of course, the gift of wisdom from the Holy Spirit, but that's different from the wisdom necessary for preaching. The preacher should always remember that the *gift* of wisdom goes before the work of wisdom. The early Dominican Humbert of Romans put it this way: "Though a grace of preaching is strictly had by God's gift, a sensible preacher still ought to do what he can to ensure that his preaching is commendable, by carefully studying what he has to preach."[4] Ordination and the gifts of the Spirit enable deeper intellectual life; they don't credential it. The gift of wisdom inaugurates the virtues of learning and docility, beginning the life of wonder and study, not ending it (*CCC*, 1831).

In the Rite of Ordination, the bishop asks the man soon to be ordained a priest if he is "*resolved* to exercise the ministry of the word worthily and wisely."[5] That is, the bishop asks him to commit to the work of study and reflection, to all it takes to preach eloquently as well as wisely. At ordination, the bishop no longer cares what a seminarian accomplished in the past, but only about what he will do in the future. The bishop asks him to take up the work of wisdom, because such wisdom is not presumed in the laying on of hands. It's work each preacher must deliberately embrace.

Although, as the Second Vatican Council taught, the Church is "by the will of Christ the teacher of truth" (*Dignitatis Pope Hamanae*, 14), and although in her voice is also the "voice of Jesus Christ," as St. John Paul II put it, a great many people, including many Catholics, just don't believe it (*Veritatis Splendor*, 64, 117). The world has changed. As Hannah Arendt said once, it's no longer possible to ask what authority is, only what *was* authority.[6] The Church today, like other bearers of traditions, has lost much of the power of her voice, and even intelligible use of many of her words. The Christian story, the teachings of Jesus, the claims of the Church: all of them are either explicitly belittled or politely ignored.

Of course, we can easily blame this aversion to the voice of the Church on our primeval enemies—that is, the world, the flesh, the devil, and the undemanding glamor of error. However, for us to refuse some of the blame for this would be to refuse the full truth. We can indeed point to the general decline of belief in the Western world, the rise of secularism, shallow trendy atheism, materialism, relativism, and any other evil "-ism" you can think of, for rising disinterest in the faith. But to refuse to look at ourselves, the quality and character of our witness, is to refuse exactly what we need to understand so that we may do the work necessary to be better evangelists for the faith. Looking only outward and not inward is exactly what we preachers should avoid.

We must candidly admit, as Dietrich Bonhoeffer did in his day, that often the Church's "preaching of Jesus Christ has been feeble and her public worship has been lifeless."[7] Too much preaching today is simply unprepared, trite, sentimental, conventional, or given lazily off the cuff, the meager offering of "irresponsible or indolent improvisation."[8] Too often it's painfully clear that the preacher isn't a reader of any real measure but is instead unreflective—that the homilist hasn't employed any noticeable mental energy that would warrant taking up another person's time.

This is why we preachers need to take up again the work of wisdom that eloquence and effective evangelization requires. We must stand in the pulpit while conscientiously standing within the wisdom of the Church, the wisdom of the great preachers who've gone before us, standing even within the wisdom of the world. We preachers must, as John Paul II said, be able to hold our own in the new "Aeropagus" of modernity (*Redemptoris Missio*, 37–38). Homilists must let go of plainly false humility, the charade of folksy simplicity, which serves only to tell the congregation that they don't need to think very much about the faith either, because, of course, the preacher hasn't.

Now this doesn't mean the preacher should become a snob, offering his people erudite, condescending lectures week after week. If the only alternative to folksy false humility is patronizing arrogance, we should just stay folksy and shallow. No, what I mean by saying we need to take seriously the work of wisdom is that we need to cultivate depth within ourselves so that we may express the depth of the faith. We must work to evoke wonder, which is the beginning of philosophy and the beginning of any real search for truth and God.[9] God is always more than we can experience, more than we can say. That's why our preaching should always evoke that sense of more, seducing and inviting listeners to desire more, luring them thereby into the infinite of God. This is what I mean by depth and wisdom. And it's what's missing from so many pulpits today.

# Our Intellectual Call

The preacher must accept the call to be a public intellectual, without either false bravado or false simplicity. The homilist should follow through on the promise made at ordination to prepare properly for the ministry of the Word, "worthily and wisely." In other ancient words, the preacher should attend to wisdom and eloquence, those eternal necessities of worthwhile preaching.

But what do I mean by calling the preacher a public intellectual? The idea comes from Václav Havel, the late playwright, dissident, and later president of the Czech Republic. As writer-turned-politician, he well understood the role, and more importantly the responsibility, of the intellectual. Talking to writers about their need to engage the wider world, his appeal could just as easily have been addressed to preachers:

> To me, an intellectual is a person who has devoted his or her life to thinking in more general terms about the affairs of the world and the broader context of things. Of course, it is not only intellectuals who do this. But intellectuals do it—if I may use the word—professionally. That is, their principal occupation is studying, reading, teaching, writing, publishing, addressing the public. Often—though certainly not always!—this makes them more receptive toward general issues; often—though by far not always!—it leads them to

embrace a broader sense of responsibility for the state of the world and its future.[10]

The world, he said, is desperate for unabashed intellectuals who see their task "to perceive far more profoundly than others the general context of things, to feel a general sense of responsibility for the world, and to articulate publicly this inner experience."[11] Their task is to see, to think, and to speak the truth. It's what Aleksandr Solzhenitsyn said of writers and artists—and it's true for preachers too—that it's the task of the intellectual "TO CONQUER THE LIE!"[12]

If preachers aren't to be intellectuals in this sense, I'm not sure what else they're to be. Almost perfectly, Solzhenitsyn and Havel's definition of an intellectual defines the preacher: a person who Sunday by Sunday speaks publicly to large, diverse congregations, speaking hopefully from within a "broader context of things"—namely, the Gospel—and with a sense of responsibility for the world and the future insofar as we hope to live the Gospel, conquering the lie. It's a task that demands the preacher possess and exercise a broad and curious mind, articulating the faith in dialogue with a broad range of human interests and concerns.

Our best preachers have always been intellectuals. From Origen's "spoiling the Egyptians" to Augustine's reminder that all truth, "wherever they may find it," belongs to God; from the sermons of Dr. Martin Luther King Jr., filled not only with beautiful, old black spirituals and scripture but also with the insights of Plato, Ovid, and St. Thomas Aquinas, to the homilies of Bishop Robert Barron, so keenly in touch with not only contemporary culture but also with the best of contemporary theology and philosophy—our tradition is full of examples of what homiletics can be when preachers take seriously their intellectual vocation.[13]

Many of our Protestant brothers and sisters in ministry are beginning to take their intellectual call more seriously. Evangelical theologians Kevin Vanhoozer and Owen Strachan have called upon pastors to rediscover and embrace their ancient, biblical, and rightful roles as public theologians and intellectuals. For too long pastors have imagined themselves belonging to the "helping professions" alongside therapists, social workers, psychologists, and psychiatrists. "But this was precisely the problem," they point out, and it's one of the reasons why pastors have backed themselves into irrelevance. If you claim to belong to the helping professions, they say, "then you had better be prepared to say what kind of help you have to give." And what can pastors say and do that others aren't saying and doing better and with more expertise?[14]

No, the proper role of the pastor, they argue, is that of public "pastor-theologian" and intellectual. The pastor's task is "to speak meaningfully and truthfully about broad topics of ultimate concern."[15] It's to be an intellectual "who knows how to relate big truths to real people."[16]

But again, I'm not talking about the snobbery of feigned intelligence. I'm talking about the intellectual depth required of a preacher charged with presenting the depth of the faith in order to solicit spiritual and theological wonder within the hearts and minds of listeners.

We must let go of our anti-intellectual embarrassment and the charade of humility, which is really just an excuse for mental laziness. It's done little but give people the impression that the Gospel is shallow and unimportant. Embracing theology and the intellectual work of ministry, as Vanhoozer insists, "is not a luxury, an optional extra (like leather trim), but a standard operating feature (like a steering wheel)."[17] The stakes of the New Evangelization demand it. We must embrace our role as public intellectuals and theologians without apology. Because the Gospel is more intriguing than we've been leading people to believe.

# Habits of Intelligence

If we're serious about the renewal of preaching, then we must renew within ourselves the habits of intelligence. And by this I mean a few practical things, habits each of us should form as part of the daily rhythm of parochial life. These are small things, which in time will make a big difference, not only in the pulpit but in all areas of life and ministry.

*First, preachers should be readers.* Thomas Long said it well that a "preacher in our time and place who does not read widely is like a physician, an attorney, or a teacher who does not read: quickly obsolete."[18] John Chrysostom said preachers should "know the arts of all."[19] If we can relay the whole narrative arc of our favorite television series—*Game of Thrones*, for instance—with all the details, twists, and turns, but can relate only a little about, say, the Gospel of Mark, then as preachers we have a problem that needs addressing. To be faithful to our vocation, to the promise to serve the ministry of the Word "worthily and wisely," we must, with regularity, turn off the television, put down the phone, and open a book—a real book and not some digital look-alike. We should read, and read a lot, every day.

But we should take care to read well. As Henry David Thoreau said, "Read the best books first, or you may not have a chance to read them at all."[20] Although the idea of a "literary canon" is, among some, complex if not controversial, it is still useful for people such as preachers. There are books with which we all should be familiar—texts, poems, and plays we ought to know, classics of the great cultural traditions from which so many preachers have for so long drawn so much treasure. Dostoevsky, Dickens, Shakespeare, Homer, Bunyan, Yeats: these and more should be in every preacher's study. But homilists also ought to explore the literary traditions of the cultures they serve—the histories, folktales, poetry, and biographies from across the world, but which may have roots in their parishes. Even if people in the congregation know little of these traditions themselves, they still have been formed by them and their idioms. Likewise, we should open ourselves to women writers. And not just the women of our tradition such as Julian of Norwich, St. Thérèse of Lisieux, and Flannery O'Connor, but also writers such as Mary Wollstonecraft, Virginia Woolf, Marilynne Robinson, and others. Embracing the literary canons of the world is not about being smart but about learning the deep language of people's hearts, about discovering *pathos*. Because even in this screened social media age, no one can speak the language of the heart as well as the person immersed in the literatures of cultures.

But preachers ought also to read outside their intellectual ken, cultivating personal interests beyond religion or literature. For example, as odd as it may seem, on Sundays I normally don't read anything theological. Immersed in scripture and theology most of the week, on Sunday my rest is to read books on economics, politics, history, poetry, and even the odd detective story. To stay current with what's going on in various corners of the world of thought, I've found podcasts invaluable. *TED Talks, Freakonomics, Radiolab, The Book Review* by the *New York Times*, and more, all provide easy entry into what the rest of the world is reading, thinking, and wondering. As hard as it is today to stay current with all the many issues, arguments, and discoveries in the world, podcasts can help keep preachers in the conversations of contemporary culture. Also, because the preacher's ministry is properly parochial, local newspapers remain invaluable. To speak to people within a community, a homilist needs to know what's going on. Even today, local newspapers provide an intimacy and depth unlike any other medium.

*And second, preachers should develop relationships outside the Church, outside their ministerial orbit.* Of course, preachers' relationships with ministers of other denominations as well as leaders of other faiths are vital, but so too are friendships and acquaintances beyond the normal avenues of religion. Hobbies, societies, and sports all provide opportunities to meet people who will both enrich the life of the preacher and challenge it.

One of my best friends, for instance, is a police officer. Both of us serve each other not only by simply being friends but also by listening to each other and even questioning each other from vocationally and institutionally different perspectives. He's not a priest, and I'm not a cop, and that's what makes our friendship so interesting. I'm also friends with lawyers, newspaper editors, and sports broadcasters. Our friendships broaden my experience and understanding, my mind and heart. They help me discover *pathos* that exists outside my religious and spiritual bubble, fostering broader understanding and empathy.

Broad reading and broad relationships are the habits of intelligence that each preacher should strive to form. This is good advice for all people, but for the preacher it's vital, producing at least two positive results.

First, broad reading and broad relationships broaden preaching. As Fred Craddock said, such breadth "will protect the parishioners from excessive influence of the minister's own opinions, prejudices, and feelings."[21] A small mind makes for small preaching, but as Phillips Brooks put it, broadness of mind saves both preacher and people from "the monotonous narrowness of one eternally repeated sermon."[22]

Preachers who are unaware of broader thought are unaware of the limits of their own. Their thinking is small, and so too is their preaching. Naturally, such a homilist will be unable to recognize that fact, the mind having never wandered beyond the fences of the familiar. Small-minded preaching becomes centered either upon the self or upon the latest petty ecclesiastical happening, the preacher incredulous of the fact that most people care little about either. This type of preaching simply becomes irrelevant, a sad offering of trite religious tropes utterly detached from the lives of listeners. The lack of relevance is painfully obvious to listeners, but small-minded preachers just don't see it and they continue to preach to people who've just stopped listening.

Second, embracing the habits of intelligence will in time offer the preacher what John Henry Newman called "a connected view." Such, he said, was the mark of "a truly great intellect," a person who "takes a connected view of old and new, past and present, far and near, and which has insight into the influence of all these one on another."[23] Or, to put it as Wendell Berry did, forming habits of intelligence will allow a homilist to know "what things are more important than other things."[24] Seeing how the Gospel speaks to the whole, how Christ speaks to the world, the preacher will see the mission and its scope more clearly. Becoming a better, more intelligent preacher, people will be more willing to listen. Because they'll want to hear what the homilist has to say, because it's thoughtful.

But it's not about winning arguments. St. Paul, for example, didn't win much by preaching in the Aeropagus. In fact, he was laughed at, collecting at the end of it only a few converts (see Acts 17:32–34). Jesus as well, if you think about it, at the end of his earthly ministry, didn't win over the scribes and Pharisees either. Rather, they simply stopped asking him questions (see Mt 22:46). At the end of Matthew's gospel, debate gives way to denunciation, talk of the tribulation, and then the Passion. For preachers, the lesson of the gospels is clear: we shouldn't overestimate either our skills or the hardness of hearts. Being an intellectual preacher is not about proving people wrong or being the smartest person in the room. Instead, it's about preaching the Gospel as credibly as one can to an incredulous world. As I'll suggest later, preaching is not about arguing ourselves out of crucifixion but rather about provoking it. Ultimately, preaching is more about witness than winning, no matter how smart we are.

And finally—it must be repeated—I'm not calling upon preachers to embrace the conceits of shallow wit and arrogance. I'm simply asking my fellow preachers to embrace the demanding work of wisdom so that we may better evoke that wonder that is the beginning of faith in the truth, which is God. For young preachers as well as old, again to quote John Paul II, to be "intellectually prepared" for the ministry of the word in the contemporary world, one must be committed to the life of the mind "for the rest of one's life."[25] This is what we must take up if we preachers are to rise above all the banalities that conspire against thoughtfulness and truth. As Albert Camus said, "we must save intelligence."[26] Amid all the shallow voices, which are so many today, we must strive to be different. Our words must have depth, for the sake of wisdom and for the sake of wonder. Because that's how a preacher credibly tells of a wondrous God.

# 2.

# THE COMMUNION
# OF PREACHERS

Therefore, since we are surrounded by so great a cloud
of witnesses . . .

—Hebrews 12:1

If the wicked speak well, why not the righteous? This was Augustine's
view of the matter, and the reason he thought preachers should be
practiced in the art of rhetoric. It's why he ended his famous book *De
Doctrina Christiana* (*Teaching Christianity*) on the subject, because it was
evangelically important.

Yet the good bishop was also realistic. He understood that the
demands of ministry afforded little opportunity for the leisured study
of rhetoric. This is why he suggested only the young study it formally,
"those who are not yet busy with more urgent requirements, which
undoubtedly take precedence over this one."[1] And besides, formally
studying rhetoric doesn't always help, for if a person just doesn't possess
a temperament for public speaking, there is little Cicero or Aristotle can
do. Formal study would be a waste of time, counterproductive.

Still, preachers need to preach well, Augustine said. In the new
aeropagi and modern marketplaces of ideas, amid the competitive swirl
of falsehood and truth, the Gospel demands ready advocates able to
preach, ready to speak about the hope inside them (see 1 Pt 3:15). If

not formally educated, preachers still must be prepared. But how? Here Augustine's advice was simple and practical. He said, "Given a bright and eager disposition, eloquence will come more readily to those who read and listen to eloquent speakers than to those who pore over the rules of eloquence."[2] This, he believed, would prepare preachers more efficiently, especially those already in ministry. "Him I much prefer to send off to read or listen to eloquent speakers and to practice imitating them, rather than instructing him to devote his time to teachers of the art of rhetoric." For Augustine that meant reading Paul and Old Testament prophets such as Amos but also other preachers proven in wisdom and eloquence.[3]

# Beginning with Logos

It's great advice, and timely as ever. And Augustine knew what he was doing giving it. Reading and listening to the great preachers of the Christian tradition can help homilists improve almost every aspect of the craft, more than nearly anything else. It's an easy and quick way to become a better homilist without starting all over again.

It's ancient advice, but even in Augustine's day it was controversial. Reading others' speeches and imitating other orators was how sophists taught rhetoric in antiquity. Socrates criticized this method because it seemed to focus more on persuading people than on knowing and arguing the truth. Wouldn't it be better, Socrates asked, to know first-hand the subject about which one speaks, rather than merely memorize another person's words? A person who simply imitates another speaker doesn't really know what he or she is talking about, Socrates thought. If learning to speak well is only a matter of imitation, then what's the importance of knowledge or philosophy?[4]

Or if one is trained only in rhetoric and not in philosophy—not really knowing the truth—isn't it more likely that such a speaker will use unphilosophical rhetoric for evil instead of good? If one speaks well but without understanding, might the result be not just disingenuous but also potentially dangerous? That was Cicero's fear, warning of the danger of those who were eloquent but unwise.[5] These fears are how rhetoric got its bad reputation over the centuries. Scrutinized by philosophers, rhetoric has always been thought to be a little suspect, if not outright dangerous, because if the only goal of rhetoric is persuasion but not also truth, then it may simply become just another art of manipulation in the service of power. It's why the annals of ancient rhetoric and philosophy combine technical advice with demands that speakers be virtuous, because "one should not persuade what is debased," as Aristotle warned, something he assumed only a person rooted in truth and goodness could avoid.[6]

Augustine knew this danger and agreed. Speaking only borrowed words, a preacher wouldn't know what to say if, to persuade, more was required. If the preacher had only a script memorized and not also knowledge of truth, he would be unprepared. In this, the philosophers were right: what sustains speech is truth. Truly to be a preacher, a person must possess knowledge, not just mouth it. As Aristotle said, persuasion requires *logos*, by which he meant the arguments that manifest truth.[7]

So Socrates was right: knowledge is indispensable for rhetoric. The Church has never disagreed. Although speech may be "beggarly" and "verbal composition simple," John Chrysostom said, still the preacher mustn't be ignorant of doctrine.[8] Christians have always believed that truth sustains speech, that "in the beginning was the Word" (Jn 1:1). For us, Christ is not only the *Logos* of all creation but also the *logos* of all speech. It's why Augustine equated being wise with knowing scripture, putting Christ and the Bible at the heart of preaching.[9] Preaching, the Second Vatican Council declared, is "nourished and regulated" by scripture (*Dei Verbum*, 21). It's how Christ stands at "the center of every homily" (*Verbum Domini*, 59). To be one with Christ is the first rule of preaching, to be intentionally aware of his presence, possessed of the *logos* of the *Logos*. Before daring to speak, we preachers should *know* the Lord in the true theological sense of the term. We should possess that knowledge that is the fruit of union before it's the fruit of information, going nowhere near a pulpit otherwise.

# The Company of Preachers

Still, imitation has its place. Aristotle called it habituation, by which he meant the acquisition of virtue by doing. If a person wants to learn a craft, he thought the best way to go about it was simply by doing it: "For we learn a craft by producing the same product that we must produce when we have learned it; we become builders, for instance, by building, and we become harpists by playing the harp. Similarly, then, we become just by doing just actions, temperate by doing temperate actions, brave by doing brave actions."[10] For Aristotle, practice makes perfect. But, of course, that means that learning a craft, like learning virtue, requires a community of imitable artisans, people worth learning from.

For Christians that community is the Church, fellowship in Christ. Paul, who wrote so often about life "in Christ" (see Rom 6:11), also encouraged the Corinthians to be "imitators of me" (1 Cor 4:16). He called Timothy his "son in the Lord" because his young protégé passed on the teachings of Jesus, he said, "just as I teach them everywhere in every church" (1 Cor 4:17). He exhorted Timothy to remember his teachers (see 2 Tm 3:14). Since the beginning, ministers have formed other ministers, preachers especially. St. John Chrysostom was formed by the apostle Paul, and John Henry Newman was deeply influenced by St. Philip Neri, to name just two. This is what Augustine was tapping into, calling on preachers to read and listen to other preachers—not plagiarism, canned homilies, or mimicry, but rather habituation. He was calling on preachers to learn their craft the way Aristotle said worked best, by imitating a company of preachers.

For me, it's an ancient method I discovered pretty much by accident, learning how to preach more by imitation than study. More from nurture than nature, anything good about my preaching is the result of growing up around excellent preachers, repeatedly listening to other preachers' sermons and homilies almost ad nauseam.

Preachers made me a preacher, not books, and not just ordination. Ordination gave me the grace of being configured to Christ, "Priest, Teacher, Pastor," allowing me to be authorized to preach in the Church. But it didn't give me the habits of a preacher (*CCC*, 1585). Instead, preachers did that, those I repeatedly heard, read, and imitated. Becoming a disciple of other preachers and orators, by reading and listening to them repeatedly, I in turn became a preacher. I found my own unique voice, but a voice clearly born of a distinct company of preachers, a voice made by others.

For instance, my father, a Protestant preacher and excellent orator, gave me his many distinctive intonations and cadences of speech. Growing up, my pastor was a fiery old preacher, part professor and part prophet, his Bible always open as he preached. He taught me to stick to scripture when preaching, that the Word of God is always more captivating and challenging than anything else. And, of course, there were others: bishops, mentors, and friends. Each made their mark, either in phrasing or rhythm or tone or in the way they approached texts. Their influence was intimate and personal, and it shaped me so deeply that if you had ever heard them, you would likely also hear them in me.

But I was also influenced by preachers I never met. In high school, just beginning to own my faith, I found an old set of cassette tapes from the early 1980s, sermons by the Disciples of Christ preacher Fred Craddock. As soon as I played them, I was hooked. I listened to those tapes for years and still have them. Even today, Craddock shapes me, preaches to me. Attracted first by Craddock's homely voice and by his masterful storytelling, I was drawn into the Gospel, bumping into the truth, as it were, as I walked along with his words, discovering Jesus for myself. Of course, I didn't yet know anything about "inductive preaching," that great flowering of twentieth-century homiletics, but Craddock's tapes introduced me to it. From him I learned, as he said, that the "story is it"—that universal truths could be shared in simple narrative.[11] Craddock taught me to trust my own voice and to preach less in propositions and more in parables, as Jesus did (see Mk 4:34).

Martin Luther King Jr. belongs to my company too. In college I bought another set of cassette tapes, recordings of King's religious sermons called *A Knock at Midnight*. I listened to them almost constantly: his imaginative sermon about Paul's letter to American Christians, his sermon on the drum major instinct, and his sermon on why Jesus called a man a fool, among others. Aside from their obvious beauty, power, and rhythm, King's sermons formed me not only in the craft but also in the ethics of preaching. They taught me the responsibility of preaching—that sometimes a preacher should take a stand even when people don't like it. Often I still recall what he said to his own congregation:

> No member of Ebenezer Baptist Church called me to the ministry. You called me to Ebenezer, and you may turn me out of here, but you can't turn me out of the ministry, because I got my guidelines and my anointment from God Almighty. And *anything* I want to say, I'm going to say it from this pulpit. It may hurt somebody, I don't know about that; somebody may not agree with it. But when God speaks, who can but prophesy? The word of God is upon me like fire shut up in my bones, and when God's word gets upon me, I've got to say it, I've got to tell it all over everywhere.[12]

King taught me that preachers must sometimes be prophets, and that "any preacher who allows members to tell him what to preach isn't much of a preacher."[13] He taught me that if we want to stand in the pulpit, then we can't "stand on the sideline and mouth pious irrelevancies and sanctimonious trivialities."[14] It's still a lesson as timely now as ever.

And there are others, Church Fathers and giants of the faith: Origen, Augustine, Chrysostom, the Cappadocians, Leo the Great, Bernard of Clairvaux, Newman, John Wesley, Phillips Brooks, Charles Spurgeon, Dietrich Bonhoeffer, Walter Brueggemann, Stanley Hauerwas, William Willimon, and more. These also belong to my company of preachers. Companions, tutors, and mentors in the faith and in the pulpit, they're with me every time I preach—so much so that when I preach, I can almost hear and feel them.

There are others in my company too, not just preachers. Winston Churchill, for instance, is among them. In his wartime speeches with their rhythm and cadence, his words were powerful enough to draw the moral lines of his age. He taught me the power of words. Mobilizing an empire to take up an "ordeal of the most grievous kind" in order to fight against a "monstrous tyranny" responsible for a "dark, lamentable catalogue of human crime," Churchill showed how words could not only convict listeners but move them too, and that there are times when that's just what's needed: powerful words to inspire powerful deeds.[15]

These are but a few in my company of preachers and orators. And each preacher should have such a company. In Dante's *Paradiso*, when Thomas Aquinas introduced himself to the poet, and before introducing the other great souls in heaven near him, Aquinas said,

> I was a lamb among the holy flock
> led by Dominic along the road
> where sheep are fattened if they do not stray.[16]

It's just the sort of company each preacher should have, "fattening" and strengthening us as we mature in the ministry of preaching.

To preach well is to preach from within a broad company of preachers and orators and lovers of language, by the light of others who've spoken the truth well or who have preached Christ effectively. As Karla Bellinger rightly points out, "We are surrounded by a rich preaching tradition. The homiletic influences of our predecessors float about our heads."[17] And we should make use of this living tradition! But we should also bring into our company of preachers other voices too, including women's voices, such as Barbara Brown Taylor, Rachel Held Evans, and others. As Catholic preachers, we would only be enriched by welcoming other preachers into our company, because better than any technique or method, by becoming a student of preachers, one becomes a better preacher. Fred Craddock taught that being a student of preaching sustains the preacher during spiritual or intellectual dryness, and that it fosters self-awareness and openness to distinctive styles and methods of preaching, helping to keep delivery diverse and fresh.[18]

It's simply good practical advice. If taken up in homiletics classes, continuing formation, or as personal discipline, it would improve one's preaching. But it's more than practical too. Reading, listening to, and imitating other preachers, in everything from language to idiom and gesture to hermeneutics, helps a preacher find a voice, a voice that's one's own, but bigger. It helps the homilist preach with that authority that amazed those who first heard Jesus (see Mt 7:29). As in the previous chapter, I said we preachers should cultivate intellectual depth. What

I'm arguing for now is fraternal depth, again for the sake of showing
forth the depth of the faith, invoking for listeners that wonder that is
the beginning of the virtue of faith and the beginning of discipleship.

# The Communion of Preachers

Which brings us to the mystical part of all this. So far, we've taken
Augustine's advice in practical terms: that preachers should learn from
other preachers by reading, listening to, and imitating those proven in
wisdom and eloquence, in scripture and rhetoric. That is, preachers
should belong to a company of preachers who can form them in the
habits of preaching. But there's something more than practical about
this advice: something deeper, something spiritual and theological. And
that's because *company*—given theological reality—is also always *communion*. When the preacher speaks, it's always from within communion,
having shared in holy things and been bound together in the Spirit. The
communion of preachers isn't just about learning from some homiletic
past; rather, it's about speaking with others across time and space the
living voice of Christ.

Jesus spoke from within communion. "I say only what the Father
taught me," he insisted (Jn 8:28). His disciples were no longer called
slaves but rather friends, because, as he said of them, "I have told you
everything I have heard from my Father" (Jn 15:15). He spoke also
within the communion of the Spirit, preaching the jubilee in Nazareth
at the beginning of his ministry with the words of Isaiah: "The Spirit
of the Lord is upon me" (Lk 4:18). This communion is what gave his
words power and credibility, because, as Jesus said of himself, "The
Father who sent me has testified on my behalf" (Jn 5:37). Jesus speaks
the words of God because he is God, the Son coming from the Father
and receiving the full gift of the Spirit—he speaks from the communion
of the Trinity (see Jn 3:34).

And it's a communion open to us by the gift of the same Spirit.
Given by the Father and the Son, the Spirit too is a gift of communion,
a voice of communion speaking not his own words but only "what he
hears" (Jn 16:13). The Spirit makes a Christian's voice more than his or

her own. "For it will not be you who speak but the Spirit of your Father speaking through you" (Mt 10:20).

This, of course, is the biblical data underneath our belief in the Communion of Saints, but also what I'm calling the communion of preachers. As the *Catechism* teaches, the Communion of Saints is a communion of faith, sacraments, charisms, goods, and ultimately a communion of charity, which is Christ himself. It's what makes us "one family of God." It's a communion lived out in the "exercise of fraternal charity" between both the living and the dead in works of mercy, the intercessions of Our Lady and the saints, and so on (*CCC*, 946–959). It's the spiritual law and bond of both the Church and heaven.

It's charity that is interpersonal, eternally so. The love among the saints will never fade (see 1 Cor 13:8–13). One of the most beautiful details of Augustine's dream of heaven in the *City of God* is his notion that God will be perceived "by each one of us in each one of us, perceived in one another."[19] What our belief in the Communion of Saints suggests is that our union with God is also our union with one another. More than an aggregation of individual saints, we are truly united in a mystical solidarity we only begin to see on earth. Yet still, this side of heaven we begin to experience it, sharing in the holy things of the faith and even in one another. We call one another brother and sister, and we love and serve one another, because it's who we are, and because it's who we will be in heaven.

Now what this looks like for the preacher is what Pope Benedict XVI, when still Joseph Ratzinger, called long ago the "personality principle." Meaning simply that ministry "has never been anonymous," Ratzinger pointed out that behind all proclaimed truth is always a "Who"—that is, a person speaking. The four gospels, for instance, are significantly accorded to persons—Matthew, Mark, Luke, and John. And the letters of the New Testament are those of Paul or James or John or Peter. The pope is Peter's successor and speaks in his voice. And the bishops, instead of inheritors of a philosophy, are rather successors of apostles.[20] And this is so because truth in Christian understanding is never disincarnate but instead always personal. It's a word become flesh and then shared with others by the gift of the Spirit, through preaching, sacraments, and love. This is why Phillips Brooks's definition of preaching as "the bringing of truth through personality" stands both the test of time and theology.[21] It's why it still matters for preachers today.

Since truth is Christ, God and human in one person, then truth spoken in Christ's name is always personal. It's why we will always have preachers, and why we'll always have readers and not recordings at Mass. Because there is something sacred and essential about the *personal* mediation of truth. It's akin to the difference between reading about love and hearing someone say "I love you." God's voice still carries after all these centuries through the voices of the disciples in whom the Spirit dwells—disciples still whispering the words of God.

This, ultimately, is why belonging to a communion of preachers is important. Not only is it a practical way to develop as a preacher, but it's also how, as preachers, our voices become bigger than our own, voices mystically more than merely ours. It's how our words can become the words of God, the only voice powerful enough to bring life to the dead (see Jn 5:25).

It's how we can begin to speak again with spiritual depth, from within the cloud of witnesses, as the world so desperately needs.

# 3.

# THE PREACHER AND THE FULLNESS OF THE CHURCH

> Know this first of all, that there is no prophecy of scripture that is a matter of personal interpretation.
>
> —2 Peter 1:20

When it comes to preaching, "no one is above the Master," to quote Irenaeus quoting Christ. "Since the faith is one and the same, he who can say much about it does not add to it nor does he who says little diminish it."[1] This is an eternal rule. Abiding by it keeps the preacher Christian, failing it, a charlatan. True for Irenaeus in the second century, it's true in ours, until all preaching ends.

To be a preacher, one must be a person of the Church. Not just smart, not just a student of great preachers who've gone before, but the preacher at heart must in all respects belong to the Church. The preacher's *ethos* must be ecclesiastical. It is not enough to cherish some mere concept of orthodoxy, for to prize orthodoxy abstracted from the Church is the beginning of heresy. Rather, the preacher must love the Church deeply, wholeheartedly, with everything, even when it hurts. Otherwise, the preacher shouldn't preach, because one's words, being merely one's own, would be unworthy of the pulpit and the People of God. The religion one spoke of, being merely personal, would be false.

To quote Irenaeus again, it is the mark of Catholic truth that it is preached and taught and handed on by the Church "as having one mouth." That's why the Church, at her best, diligently and unapologetically guards her preaching. Because the living voice of the Church is also always mysteriously identifiable with the living voice of Christ.[2]

Irenaeus wrote in an age not unlike ours, full of versions of Christianity, competing theologies, and various vying opinions. It was an age not unlike Paul's, who when walking through Corinth made note of its "many 'gods' and many 'lords'" (1 Cor 8:5). It's why the title of Irenaeus's book is called (note the plural) *Against Heresies*, and why Paul said, "Yet for us there is one God, the Father . . . and one Lord, Jesus Christ" (1 Cor 8:6). What the Church has always concerned herself with is speaking truth clearly within the marketplace of ideas, within the clamor of partial truths and seductive falsehoods. Her concern has always been to speak in the world the clear voice of Christ, unadulterated and uncompromised.

Now, for Irenaeus, in practice, this meant two things for preachers. First, it meant obedience to the rule or canon of truth, and second, it meant obedience to apostolic authority. The rule of truth, of course, is creedal faith, the basic summary of scripture found in the creeds of the Church: belief in the Passion and divinity of Christ, his birth from the Blessed Virgin, his coming again in glory, and so on. This is the faith that the Church, as Irenaeus put it, "carefully guards."[3]

But as Irenaeus and so many other Church Fathers made clear, that by itself isn't enough. Creedal orthodoxy is only sustainable within the communion of the Church, particularly under the obedience of faith as it's lived within the Church under the magisterium.

In matters of dispute, for instance, Irenaeus sought the arbitration of "the most ancient Churches, those in which the apostles lived."[4] Augustine taught that the ambiguities of scripture were settled not only by a hermeneutic of charity but also by the rule of faith and the authority of the Church.[5] Truth, the Fathers understood, was inseparable from the Church; to hold one without the other, as St. Basil the Great put it, was to "fatally mutilate the Gospel."[6]

Another way to think about this is to reflect on how scripture relates to tradition in the Church. The *Catechism of the Catholic Church*, summarizing the Second Vatican Council's dogmatic constitution *Dei Verbum*, says that scripture and tradition, though distinct, are of the same source and work for the same end. Together, both make present in the Church "the mystery of Christ" (*CCC*, 80). What this means in practice is that although the People of God read and study scripture, as each member is free to do because of the common indwelling of the Holy Spirit, it is nonetheless the magisterium that is charged with the "task of giving authentic interpretation of the Word of God" (*CCC*, 85). In Catholic thought and practice, the people's reading and the Church's teaching always go together.

It's a sacramental symbiosis making a whole bigger than the sum of its parts. Scripture and tradition speak together in the voice of the Church, the one voice of Christ. From the time of Christ and Paul to Irenaeus and Augustine to today, it's how the Gospel is genuinely shared: biblically and traditionally—that is, ecclesiastically. It's how God speaks clearly in an unclear world—a divine clarity all preachers must serve.

Now this matters because what Benedict XVI said long ago about the crisis of preaching remains true today: this is in no small measure a "crisis of ecclesial consciousness."[7] "Today more than ever before," he said, "the preacher tends to place himself outside and above the believing Church," forgetting that preachers exist "*in* the Church, not over her."[8] It seems we need to learn the lessons of Irenaeus again: that no one is above the Master and that the Gospel we preach is not our own.

# A Gospel Not Our Own

But what does this mean on the ground in daily ministry, in the parish and in the pulpit?

If what Irenaeus and others taught is true, that the preacher must be a person of the Church, then the homilist must be a person of scripture and tradition, a person whose intellect and will is consecrated to the work of the Gospel in the mission of the Church. Consecrated practically and daily, in every detail of ministry, and not just in theory or in sentiment, the preacher's dedication to the Church's essential work must be total.

This means the preacher must be a student of the Bible, reading and praying with scripture regularly and not just during the Liturgy of the Hours or homily preparation. If, as the Church teaches, preaching should be "nourished and ruled by sacred Scripture" (*Dei Verbum*, 21). then sacred scripture should nourish and rule the preacher as well as the preacher's day. As busy as we priests and other clergy are, we shouldn't be too busy for the Bible. Bound to the promise made at ordination to be scriptural persons, exercising the ministry of the Word worthily and wisely, we preachers must make serious engagement with scripture a daily habit. Amid all the meetings and appointments and visits in the day, we shouldn't fear blocking out considerable time for the Bible. By regularly studying scripture, leading a Bible study, or even—scandalous as it may sound to some—attending a Bible study led by a layperson in the parish, engaging scripture ought to be our normal modus operandi.

Consider how preaching might be different in the Catholic Church if we priests and deacons came together to study scripture and not just to check the Mass schedule. St. Gregory the Great said that he often came to understand scripture only when placed in the middle of his brethren.[9] Wouldn't our homilies be a bit more coherent, a bit richer? What if the priest's office wasn't called an office or workspace but rather a study? Might not even administrative tasks bear a more sacred productivity? What would our preaching look like if we broke the constraining pro-fessionalized mold of modern ministry? What would our ministry look like if we lived and worked as if studying scripture was more important than almost anything else?

Benedict XVI gives us an idea. In his exhortation *Verbum Domini*, he called upon all members of the clergy to hear the Word before speaking the Word, a thoroughly traditional invitation. By approaching scripture frequently with supple, prayerful hearts, allowing scripture to penetrate thought and emotion, Pope Benedict's hope was that clergy would begin to reflect the Gospel by their very existence (*Verbum Dommi*,

79–80).Frequent study, but also frequent prayer—particularly lectio divina—when carried out in everyday ministry places the preacher in the presence of the Lord, a presence akin to the Eucharist. This in turn inspires *actio*, the authentic work of the believer, in this case the preacher (*Verbum Dominin*, 87). Now we'll say more about this in a later chapter, but suffice it to say here, the reason Benedict XVI emphasized this type of engagement with scripture was that he believed it helps make the preacher's personal voice more like the voice of the Church and the voice of scripture. Practically speaking, serious study of scripture and lectio divina is how the preacher accomplishes the symbiosis of the personal and ecclesial voice.

But as in theology, so also in ministry, *sola scriptura* is insufficient for the preacher. Again, a person of the Church must be scriptural *and* ecclesiastical, consciously and consistently offering one's voice to the voice of the hierarchical Church. "The preacher does not preach on his own behalf or on behalf of any particular congregation or of any other group but, rather, on behalf of the Church, which is one in all places and at all times."[10] Scripture is liturgical and public before it's personal, and even then, it's personal only insofar as it belongs to the Church's tradition. That's what the writer of the Second Letter of Peter was saying, that his interpretation bore authority not only because he was an "eyewitness" of God's majesty but also because it was an interpretation in harmony with prophets and apostles, even Paul (see 2 Pt 1:16; 1:21; 3:2; 3:15). It's simply not possible to be fully biblical without also being ecclesiastical, because it's impossible to consider scripture without considering other people.

Now in practice this means for the preacher obedience. Not just theoretical, but obedience that is daily and detailed. It means ecclesiastical obedience. It means clear obedience to the teachings and teachers of the Church, the Holy Father and the bishops in communion with him. The point is not trivial. Simone Weil once said that obedience was the "necessary food of the soul," and that whoever is "deprived of it is ill."[11] This is true for the preacher as much as anyone. The Gospel simply cannot be preached by the disobedient.

But what does obedience mean in the parish? For deacons and paro-chial vicars, it means refraining from controversial topics in homilies without first consulting the pastor, without seeking permission. For the pastor, it means being mindful of the bishop's mind and the minds of the other bishops of the Church. It means refraining from criticism, airing whatever disagreements one may have, whether about doctrine or ethics or anything else. We preachers must be very careful about tackling controversy in homilies, and we must never criticize bishops or the pope from the pulpit, no matter how right we think we are, and no matter how right we may in fact be. To be honest, in a time of scandal this can be very difficult. But St. Gregory of Nazianzus warned of the danger of this centuries ago, how public bickering and dissent weap-onized the enemies of Christ, putting the Church on stage, subjecting her to ridicule.[12] To preach out of tune with the Church belittles truth and weakens the power of her witness. That's why such dissent simply has no place in the pulpit, no matter how strongly we may feel. Because even if we're right, we've still besmirched the Church. We've only given people reason to discount her and not take her seriously about anything. And that's just too high a cost simply for being right.

But it's not just about the Church's public witness, saving institution-al face. What's at stake is deeper than that. Once we offer from the pulpit our utterly personal view on any one matter, suddenly we're preaching *our* Christ and *our* Catholicism. Suddenly, we're inviting listeners into *our* communion and not the communion of the Church.

It's a narrowing of communion common among the heterodox and heretical, among those who've made the pulpit a sideshow for their one or two pet issues or their tired grievances against the Church. But it's not just among them. Sometimes you'll come across a priest who's been really taken by some aspect of theology—let's say divinization. Suddenly every homily preached is about divinization. Not a single verse fails to illumine some point of the theology of divinization—every reading, every Sunday, eventually boring the People of God with divinization.

Of course, boredom is preferable to heresy, but still, for the preacher to emphasize personal theological preferences, whether silly or sane, is a genuine problem. That's because, fundamentally, in some measure it betrays the Church and the singular voice of Christ, which the Church alone authoritatively speaks. Preachers may speak the voice of Christ, but they don't arbitrate it. We may be Christ's messengers, but Christ certainly isn't ours. That's the proper order of things, the line of communication, which homilists should remember. The two elements of preaching may be truth and personality, but still, truth comes first.[13] Never is truth made an instrument of the preacher, but rather the preacher is always the instrument of truth.

Yet sometimes the preacher may be called to fulfill the role of prophet. None of what I have said about obedience excludes this. The fire shut up in the bones of Jeremiah may burn within even the humblest priest or deacon, and there is little that can or should be done to snuff out such fire (see Jer 20:9). So long as the Spirit dwells among us, prophecy will be part of the Church, and it's quite possible even in these days that some preachers will be called to be prophets. There are no proper channels for it, no legitimacy other than its own truth and power, so each preacher must simply be open and ready. Because the Spirit is truly democratic, speaking through whomever he pleases, not just official spokespersons.

But the preacher should be careful before assuming the prophet's mantle. As Yves Congar wrote, "It's great to be a prophet, but only if one really is one."[14] There is about real prophetic ministry a necessary tension, even necessary conflict, which must arise between the prophet and the rest of the Church—tension equally providential and painful. Jeremiah was beaten and imprisoned by Pashhur, the priest (see Jer 20:1–2). He was marginalized and ridiculed. The preacher sensing the prophet's call should ponder that, deeply and in prayer, because if the call is from God, it'll likely look like that. That is, the would-be preacher-prophet must understand that the immediate reward for his prophesying will not be praise but rather suffering.

Yet even if the preacher says something true and is subsequently ridiculed and marginalized, that doesn't mean the prophecy making is genuine. What separated St. Francis from Martin Luther, for example—or even a great prophetic preacher such as Savonarola from Philp Neri—wasn't only theology but—just as importantly—ecclesiastical obedience. What characterizes true prophetic preaching is submissive love for the Church, however unmodern that sounds. It's love like the kind found among the saints—like Thomas Aquinas, for example, who just before his death submitted everything he taught to the "judgement of the Holy Roman Church."[15] What separates the merely egotistical from the ecclesiastical, the charlatan from the prophet, is the willingness to be judged by the Church. Again, to quote Congar, "The only valid prophecy in the church is in the service of the church's apostolicity."[16] The point is that to speak truth as a preacher, even prophetically, one must always speak to build up the Church and her mission and never to destroy it, even her hierarchical and institutional elements. No matter how fiery the prophetic word may be, it must still be a word of healing and restoration.

In this epoch of individualism, which is at root what likely most often corrupts the prophetic, we preachers must dare to submit to the Church in a radical, and radically illiberal, way. Because no matter the value of our contemporary understanding of personal autonomy, if we're open to the prophetic, as we preachers must be, then as Paul made clear, our prophetic preaching must always build up the Church and never destroy or deconstruct it (see 1 Cor 14:3–4). We must be preachers for the Church, not for ourselves. To be a preacher of any sort, ordinary or prophetic, we must be radically ecclesiastical.

# Farmer and Mother

That's not all. Not just a matter of scripture and ecclesiastical obedience, again, preaching is also a matter of communion, particularly the communion we preachers share with the whole People of God, the laity. Only in real communion with the lay faithful can the preacher experience the fullness of the Church, becoming truly a person of the Church. Without real communion with the laypeople of the Church, the preacher's experience of the Church simply isn't real. It's mystically sterile, showing in the shallowness of preaching.

It's the sort of shallow sterility described in Wendell Berry's novel *Jayber Crow*. The preachers that passed through the fictional town of Port William were detached, aloof souls, never drawing near the people, never staying long enough to develop actual relationships with people in the community. Jayber, the village barber and protagonist, describes the preaching he experienced in the fictional Port William, a kind of preaching that is sadly sometimes all too real in today's Church:

> The sermons, mostly, were preached on the same theme I had heard over and over at The Good Shepherd and Pigeonville: We must lay up treasures in Heaven and not be lured and seduced by this world's pretty and tasty things that do not last but are like the flower that is cut down. The preachers were young students from the seminary who wore, you might say, the mantle of power but not the mantle of knowledge. They wouldn't stay long enough to know where they were, for one thing. Some were wise and some were foolish, but none, so far as Port William knew, was ever old. They seemed to have come from some Never-Never Land where the professionally devout were forever young. They were not going to school to learn where they were, let alone the pleasures and the pains of being there, or what ought to be said there. You couldn't learn those things in a school. They went to school, apparently, to learn to say over and over again, regardless of where they were, what had already been said too often. They learned to have a very high opinion of God and a very low opinion of His works—although they could tell you that this world had been made by God Himself.[17]

Preaching divorced from people and place, it's what's offered by homilists who don't listen to the People of God and creation with reverence. That's Berry's point. It's the sort of preaching that is the product of those of us who don't understand or respect the intimate communion between preacher and people and community and land.

The Bible, however, offers a different way to think about preacher and people. Biblical images describing the communion of preacher and people are organic and beautiful—images of seed, fertilization, and fruitfulness, the human voice, and birth and family. It's Isaiah's imagery:

> Yet just as from the heavens
> > the rain and snow come down

And do not return there
> till they have watered the earth,
> making it fertile and fruitful,
Giving seed to the one who sows
> and bread to the one who eats,
So shall my word be
> that goes forth from my mouth;
It shall not return to me empty,
> but shall do what pleases me,
> achieving the end for which I sent it. (Is 55:10–11)

Seed and soil and growth: this is also the imagery Jesus used in his parables, the seed being the "word of the kingdom" (Mt 13:19). And the seed is sown, to mix metaphors, by the "voice of the Son of God," which to hear is to live (Jn 5:25). The "word of truth, the gospel," is something that bears fruit and grows (Col 1:5–6). It's a word, to mix metaphors yet again, that gives birth. At Athens, Epicureans and Stoics called Paul a *spermologos*, which they meant to be an insult, but which he may have taken as a compliment (see Acts 17:18). For Paul saw himself in just those terms, describing his ministry in terms of pregnancy and parenting, of being "in labor until Christ [is] formed" in his people, caring for them "as a nursing mother cares for her children" (Gal 4:19; 1 Thes 2:7). These are the primal images of the communion of preacher and people, that of the seed of God's Word and the fertile soil of minds and hearts, the fertilization of new life in the womb of the Body of Christ.

Pope Francis used this same imagery, reminding us that "the Church is a mother, and that she preaches the same way that a mother speaks to her child." Homilies are like family conversations, he said, filled with a "spirit of love," even though they may sometimes be "tedious." Yet they still "bear fruit, in due time, in the hearts of her children" (*Evangelii Gaudium*, 139–140).

This then, clearly, is how we preachers ought to think about our relationship to the people who listen to us, not in terms of credentialed expertise, but instead with these earthy, organic, and family images. These are not the imagery of lecturer or salesperson, nor even the images of physician or coach; rather, they are the images of farmer and mother, which better describe the relationship between preacher and people.

There are, of course, other images and metaphors for the preacher. In the Early Church, some suggest, the image of the physician was most common.[18] Thomas Long in *The Witness of Preaching* surveys other common images: that of preacher as "herald," "pastor," "storyteller/poet" and "witness."[19] Each image expresses some aspect of preaching, each valuable for what it emphasizes about the preaching event. However, none capture the sense of communion that binds together preacher and people quite like the images of farmer and mother. That's because these images imply lasting bonds: the farmer with the land, the mother with her child. The farmer who plants seed must first till the soil, then seed at just the right time, water at just the right time, and finally practice patience and trust in the growth, which at first is invisible. For the mother, conception begins in love. As the child grows within her, she prepares herself for a motherhood that will grow and change just as her child grows and changes: feeding and teaching and guiding at first in one way and then in another. The reason these images are so important, and why preachers should keep them in mind and imagination, is because, better than other images of the preacher, these foster virtues suited to good preaching—gentleness, patience, and mercy. They keep the preacher from bruising the reed and snuffing out the small, struggling flame (see Is 42:3).

Yet this isn't paternalism. We should be careful to avoid that sort of condescension that is rightly dismissed, when in tone, manner, and words, the preacher assumes authority as if by right, but that neither contemporary society nor the people have granted. Whether the homilist really bears this authority or not, it matters little if the people listening won't accept it. And it's understandable when they don't accept it, especially if the preacher hasn't taken the time to discern or respect the Spirit present among the People of God. It's one thing to see the People of God in terms of passive soil and little children, but it's quite another to forget they have brains, that they must be persuaded and not just told, and that they stand as free people before the Word of God just as freely as the preacher.

Along with the image of farmer and mother, the preacher should remember the words of Paul, that "we were all given to drink of one Spirit" (1 Cor 12:13). When we dare to preach, we mustn't forget that the Holy Spirit dwells "in the Church *and* in the hearts of the faithful," in us as well as in the people listening (*Lumen Gentium*, 4; emphasis added). The truth we speak, the Holy Spirit, which has been poured into the People of God, speaks to them too—and often more intimately and effectively than we can (see Rom 5:5). This theological reality demands not only respect but also reverence. It demands that we understand that Christ already dwells in the hearts of those to whom we preach, and that we can find him there—if we're humble enough.

We shouldn't forget that it was a layperson, a woman, Mary Magdalene, who first witnessed the Resurrection and who preached it to the Twelve. Scripture's description of Peter's disbelief of her and the other women's testimony is not meant to be read as praise of the apostle's skepticism, but quite the opposite (see Lk 24:10–11). We should accept and look for Christ and his truth in and among the People of God. Benedict XVI taught very beautifully that persons themselves can be a sort of exegesis of scripture—that holiness itself is an interpretation of the Bible (*Verbum Domini*, 48–49, 83). That is, in studying scripture in light of the lives of the saints, the meaning of scripture is sometimes unlocked and deepened. Now this must be true not only of the great saints of history but also of some of the saints sitting in our pews.

And that means when Pope Francis invited the preacher not only to contemplate the Bible but also to "contemplate his people," he was inviting the homilist to do something more than take their collective pulse or register opinion (*Evangelii Gaudium*, 154). He was calling on the preacher to experience something deeper, something better understood in terms of communion. Calling each of us into gentle, personal dialogue with our people, what Pope Francis meant by "accompaniment" is something altogether open to the work of the Spirit, to the sacred that exists within both preacher and people. Calling on each of us to "remove our sandals before the sacred ground of the other," Francis was inviting us to discover the spiritual reality that exists in and between clergy and laity. He was asking us to see how the Spirit dwells always in both and how that's beautiful—and how it shouldn't frighten but instead inspire us to draw nearer to our people, making real connections that bear fruit on all sides (*Evangelii Gaudium*, 128, 169).

But what does this mean practically? Phillips Brooks wrote that sermons should "feel their hearers."[20] A curious way to put it, what he meant was that the preacher ought to have not only a heart for listeners but also awareness. Fred Craddock said the preacher "preaches *in* and *out* of as well as *to*" the community.[21] All of this implies that the preacher should be alert to the trials, tribulations, triumphs, challenges, and goings-on of listeners, and preach as if these things really exist and really matter. It's painful to experience the disconnect between preacher and congregation, when between them there is obviously little to nothing in common, when after some crisis or joy in the community, the preacher musters mere generic platitudes or a few churchy quotes, which may equally fit every congregation on earth, or none.

To preach well, we must, like Paul, "become all things to all, to save at least some" (1 Cor 9:22). The respect and reverence due to the People of God demands that we take interest in what interests them, that we try to understand their hopes and fears, and that we understand that, although their hearts innately long for God, they long for other things too. We must understand the value families place on sports, dance, and school, for instance, and all those other things that fill their lives with meaning, even when we know those things aren't nearly meaningful enough. Before we denounce the false god of youth sports or politics or ballroom dancing or bingo, we must try to understand what our people find so appealing about them. We must try to ally ourselves with what's good in them.

Today, across many disciplines, a lot of people talk about something called behavioral economics. *Nudge* by Richard Thaler and Cass Sunstein is the bestselling book that got all this started, at least popularly. Reimagining ourselves more as "choice architects" than as dictators or leaders, they said, should help us to "nudge" instead of command or rebuke, because commanding and rebuking so often simply don't work.[22] If you really want to move someone, they say, it's more about incentives than imperatives.

But, of course, preachers have been working in the field of behavioral economics for millennia. None of it's new. Consider Gregory the Great's advice to bishops:

> Wherefore, the discourse of a teacher should be adapted to the character of the hearers, so as to be suited to the individual in his respective needs, and yet never deviate from the art of general edification. For what else are the minds of his hearers but, if I may say so, the taut strings of a harp, which the skillful harpist plays with a variety of strokes, that he may not produce a discordant melody? And it is for this reason that the strings give forth a harmonious melody, because they are not plucked with the same kind of stroke, though plucked with one plectrum. Hence, too, every teacher, in order to edify all in the one virtue of charity, must touch the hearts of his hearers by using one and the same doctrine, but not giving to all one and the same exhortation.[23]

Now this is nothing more than a patristic version of the nudge. Gregory wrote at length about how to exhort both the smart and the dull, the proud and the humble, the sincere and the insincere, and almost every other sort of person imaginable. The point is that preachers should be alert to their listeners, psychologically and socially adept to their emotions and thinking, and know how to react. As we'll discuss in a later chapter, preachers must be alert to *pathos*, for only then could a homilist ever hope to persuade and nudge listeners toward Christ.

For without respect for *pathos*, things can backfire. Once, the famous and somewhat scandalous French actress Sarah Bernhardt toured the States, drawing large crowds everywhere she went. The Episcopal bishop of Chicago at the time thought it best to confront this salacious threat to the morality of his flock head-on. Preaching against her, taking out ads, he warned his people of the danger of her performance. Yet despite his efforts, she came and went, and the crowds in Chicago were as big as any. Leaving town, her manager wrote the bishop to thank him and enclosed a check for $200. He was grateful, he wrote, for all the advertising the bishop provided![24]

That's why the nudge is better. People aren't passive idiots but instead free individuals, and so preachers must be smart about how they confront the good, the bad, and the ugly in society. People demand respect and reverence, accompaniment, and patience, even those unformed or hostile. We must realize that people will only listen to us if first they believe we've listened to them, genuinely and respectfully.

But to do this the preacher must stand nimbly between God and the world, balanced on faith in the midst of the people. Resisting both sanctimonious isolation on the one hand and complete worldliness on the other, the preacher seeks that faithful space between this world and the next, between truth and error. Augustine wrote about this, how Christian leaders should conduct themselves among those who've "not yet learned to live by dying." He said, "It seems to us that unless we in some small degree conform to them in regard to those very things from which we desire to see them delivered, we shall not succeed in doing them any good." However, he said we should be careful not to weigh ourselves down with the "mire of this world."[25] A precarious balance, it's the sort of equilibrium preachers must work hard to maintain: the ability to empathize without losing the ability to inspire.

But again, all of this is for the sake of something deeper, something more than being merely relevant or engaging. If the proper imagery of preaching is fruitfulness and growth—the imagery of farmer and mother—and if that implies that the soil of the lay faithful is rich and the womb of the People of God is fertile, then it must mean that real preaching helps bring about new life, a new birth or the sprout of a seedling.

That is, born of people and preacher is a unique creation, the birth of an unbegotten word. The voice of Christ speaks in the voice of the hierarchical Church, through the preachers of the Church, a voice that finds an echo in the hearts and minds and voices of the laity. The first voice, as Yres Congar described it, is "fatherly and fertilizing," while the second voice, "in exact agreement with the first, does not repeat it mechanically: it amplifies it, carries it further, enriches it and corroborates it."[26] This is how the mystery of Christ is made present in the world, how the voice of Christ is spoken outside the Church in the witness of preacher and people together. That is, out of the communion of preachers *and people*, and not from the mouths of preachers alone, comes the word of Christ for the world. That is the miracle of preaching: that it begins and fertilizes the word of Christ spoken by the whole Church and not just part of it, and that it's a word that inspires another word: Good News for the world.

"Shekinah is between beings," Martin Buber said once, and it describes well this miracle of preaching.[27] It's the sort of preaching that takes account of the reverence and respect due to the laity, the sort of preaching that believes in the contribution of the laity to the preaching of the Gospel in the world. To be a person of the Church, the preacher must be open to this experience: to the communion of the laity. Because it's a gift meant to complement preaching. And because the fullness of the Church cannot be experienced without it, nor the fullness of Christ.

# Vir Ecclesiasticus

This then is the heart of the preacher, the homilist's character or *ethos*. This is its final form: the preacher in communion with the whole Church. Beginning this book, I borrowed Phillips Brooks's definition of preaching—"the bringing of truth through personality"—to argue that it is with the homilist's personality that the renewal of preaching must begin, that it's the heart of the preacher that must first concern us.[28] We see now that it is the renewing of the intellectual life of the preacher, rooting him in the preacher's tradition and in the fullness of the Church, that is the final form of the preacher's heart. And that's the form of the Church, the preacher's *ethos* fully ecclesiastical.

Henri de Lubac called such a person a *vir ecclesiasticus*, what I've been calling a "person of the Church." What de Lubac described is precisely what I mean, naming succinctly the sort of heart that must beat inside the preacher today: a heart for God and the Church, for people and the world.

"He is a man in the Church," de Lubac said, "a man of the Church, a man of the Christian community." But more than his being merely institutionally loyal, "the Church will have stolen his heart."[29] The preacher of the Church will understand that ecclesiastical obedience, far from being oppressive, is instead "the most secret point in the mystery of faith."[30] Not concerned with defending one's autonomy, saving one's own voice distinct from the voice of the Church, the preacher's obedience is the same as the preacher's love for the Church. It will be the same thing as the preacher's love for Christ, whose own obedience is only to be imitated. Like the Lord's obedience, the preacher's will become a "source of eternal salvation" for others (Heb 5:9). "He will not grant himself the right to call himself a son of the Church unless he is, first of all and always, a child of the Church, and that in all sincerity," de Lubac stated. With love that is not merely theoretical and sentimental but also real, the preacher will be obedient to the magisterium of the Church, without caveat and not grudgingly.[31] Otherwise, the preacher should not preach, because the preacher doesn't love enough.

Such must be the heart of the preacher before ever writing a word, before ever opening the mouth. Before setting out on the way of the preacher, one must surrender the heart. It must become a heart that has fallen in love with Christ and with his bride, the Church.

A heart in love, set afire by the Spirit.

# PART II: REDEEMING THE WAY OF THE PREACHER

Teach your mouth to say what is in your heart.
—Abba Poemen
*The Alphabetical Sayings of the Desert Fathers*, 163

It's a lot like cosmetics and cooking, Socrates said: the sort of public speaking he called sophistry and rhetoric. He was talking about the sort of speaking lawyers and other public figures engaged in—that is, speech meant to persuade the masses. He described it this way because he didn't much care for it. He didn't respect rhetoric, because it wasn't really a true "art" (*tekhne*) in his mind, but more an acquired knack learned by experience, by trial and error. True arts, like medicine, followed rules and reason, he thought, but not rhetoric. Rhetoric was different, he said, because it was more like learning a trick.[1] It's why Socrates distrusted rhetoric, because it wasn't built upon the pure arguments of philosophy.

Aristotle, however, thought a little better of it. He said rhetoric was an art—that is, a craft, which he said was a sort of reasoned production.[2] Viewing it as a counterpart to philosophical argument, he defined rhetoric as the ability to understand the "means of persuasion." Rhetoric, he said, could be studied and taught, which explains why he gave lectures on it. And it's important, he said, because it's "useful." Rhetoric was necessary for the sake of justice, he thought, because it wasn't enough simply to know what was just; one also had to know how to persuade others to accept what was just, while at the same time be able to detect when someone was misusing rhetoric for what was unjust. For Aristotle, the good guys needed to know rhetoric too; otherwise, truth risked being overrun by error.[3]

The Christian tradition sides with Aristotle here. Yes, Jesus said to his disciples, "Do not worry beforehand about what you are to say" (Mk 13:11); and yes, Paul said that Christian witness isn't about the "word alone," but also about the power of the Holy Spirit (1 Thes 1:5). Yet, nonetheless, Christian preaching has always embraced rhetoric, even when ostensibly rejecting it. And for the same reason as Aristotle: for the sake of truth and justice against error and injustice. As Augustine asked, if the wicked use rhetoric for the sake of error, then why not the righteous as well, those who are, after all, "defending the truth"?[4]

This is why not only in the ancient Church but also in a renewed way in the modern Church, since at least the Council of Trent, the rhetoric of the Gospel—that is, preaching—has been handled like an "art" in Aristotle's sense of the term.[5] It's why the fathers of the Second Vatican Council insisted that not only should seminarians spend more time in biblical studies, but they should also be trained to deliver such knowledge effectively, "giving it expression in their speech" (*Optatam Totius*, 4).

But thinking about the rhetoric of preaching isn't just for seminarians. Rather, it would do well for all who are ordained to preach to think about the rhetoric of the ministry of the word, seeing it as part of their responsibility, tendering the proclamation of the Gospel in the most effective manner possible. This should concern all of us, no matter how long we've been ordained.

Pope Francis said preachers should devote "prolonged time" to homily preparation (*Evangelii Gaudium*, 145). The 1999 document put out by the Congregation for the Clergy, *The Priest and the Third Christian*

*Millennium*, said more and put it even more bluntly. It lamented the "irresponsible or indolent improvisation" of homilies, saying explicitly that priests should "cultivate the formal aspects of preaching," taking cue from the resurgence of the study of rhetoric in universities.[6]

The Catholic Church today has indeed made a concerted effort to improve the quality of preaching in parishes: rich teaching documents, workshops, journals, and so on. There is more on offer today for the would-be preacher than possibly at any other time in the history of the Church. Yet the dividends are still meager: Catholic preaching is still largely poor. Why?

Perhaps it's because (and I say this with all deference and due respect for my fellow clergy) we preachers need to do more *personally* to make better preaching a reality. By integrating the long-standing wisdom of preaching, both spiritual and practical, into our lives more formally and more fully, we need to abandon the "I've got this" mentality, which, frankly, too many of us have when it comes to preaching. We need to be more serious about the way we preach, about the ministry of the word that God has given us.

And that means being more serious about rhetoric, about preparation and delivery. It means being willing to accept that what we're doing (or more likely not doing) just isn't good enough. Phillips Brooks said, "Do not be tempted by the fascination of spontaneousness. Do not be misled by any delusion of inspiration."[7] But that's exactly what we've done. Many of us, if we're honest, don't prepare as we should. We preach without study or method. And we preach badly.

Out of respect for the Gospel and the People of God, this should stop. We must quit offering our people the rushed scribblings of our shallow and rushed thoughts, thinking that will do. When developing habits of preparation and methods of delivery both earnest and effective, we must stick to them, not stubbornly but faithfully. We must honor the time both God and his people give us to speak and quit taking it for granted. We should preach like it's important, like the Gospel is important, like our people are important, because clearly and sadly, we often haven't.

For younger clergy, forming good habits is critical. Habits are like wet-setting clay, Brooks said, taking shape early in a preacher's ministry.

It's important to get a good start, learning from good preachers, finding methods and styles that fit.[8] Preachers are not fully formed at ordination. Like the brains of newborns, it takes a while for them to grow to form. Younger clergy should accept this developmental fact about themselves and simply be humble enough to resist the temptation to feign wisdom they do not possess. Instead, they should just keep learning, trusting in the sure growth of wisdom and grace.

But we older priests should be humble too; humble enough, at least, to pray over the dry bones of our dry preaching. We too should be willing to reconsider our habits and methods, no matter how ingrained. For older preachers, though, it's also about personal vocational renewal, about desire and commitment for a renewed heart and renewed ways. The deadly enemy of veteran preaching is that ancient noonday demon called acedia. We older clergy need to be alert to this spiritual disease, as frightened of it as we are of physical disease. Aware of this very real danger, we older clergy should be all the more willing to pray and work for a new heart, like Ezekiel dreamed, cleansed with a new spirit for the sake of restoration (see Ez 36:25–26). We must be open to a new way of preaching, new thinking and new methods, and even to change.

This is what the second half of this book is about: redeeming the way of the preacher. Attending, as we have, to the *ethos* of the preacher, a little to the *pathos* of the People of God, and a little to the *logos* of preaching—that is, to Christ and scripture—now we turn to what Aristotle called *lexis* and *taxis* and *hypokrisis*. By *lexis*, Aristotle meant the style of speaking. By *taxis*, he meant the arrangement or order of a speech. By *hypokrisis*, he meant delivery. I call it simply the way of the preacher, the preparation and performance of preaching. For the ancients then, so also for us now, *lexis*, *taxis*, and *hypokrisis* matter; for as Aristotle said, "It is not enough to have a supply of things to say but it is also necessary to say it in the right way."[9] Or, as Gregory the Great put it, a preacher should be "orderly in his speech," preaching truth not in a "slovenly manner" but instead alert to the "practical needs of the audience."[10]

But first we must spend a little more time with *logos*, or to be more precise, with *Logos*. That is, to begin to think about the way of the preacher, we must first think about prayer. For preaching is first born of

*Logos*. And since *Logos* is the living Word, prayer is the first way of the preacher—conversing with God, as Evagrius described it—speaking with God before we ever speak with others.[11]

# 4.

# THE PREACHER
# AT PRAYER

You should pray that God may put words into your mouth.

—St. Augustine, *Teaching Christianity* 4.30.63

When Bl. Dom Columba Marmion, a saintly Benedictine monk from a century ago, wrote about prayer and the priest, he first quoted Augustine's commentary on John 15:5 where Jesus said, "Without me you can do nothing." We should notice, Augustine wrote, that Jesus didn't say "much" but instead "nothing." The point, of course, is that for the priest, regarding the need of God in prayer, "our dependence is no less absolute."[1]

Without relying on God in prayer, it's not that the priest will do less, but that he will do nothing, even if he's busy at work. No matter how alight with the Spirit a priest may seem, without prayer he will be quite literally useless, fraudulent. And as a preacher, he will be dangerous. When praying, the preacher must seek the Preacher to preach well or at all.

Without prayer, preachers are ignorant of their subject, regardless of their education or experience, and no matter what their speaking ability suggests. Without prayer, in time, it will show, because the fruit will not be there. If there isn't prayer, there isn't preaching. This is a universal truth, as immovably alpha and omega as anything this side of heaven. Yet it's a truth often taken for granted, often overlooked. It's neglected because we're so busy; we often rush through our prayers, praying poorly or sometimes not at all. All of this influences our ministry—our preaching as much as anything else.

The bishops of the United States called prayer a "non-negotiable," something that ought to be a "way of life" for preachers.[2] Here the modern Church echoes the ancient Church exactly. Pope Francis taught that we preachers should be the "first to hear the word which we preach" (*Evangelii Gaudium*, 149). It's precisely what Augustine said: that the preacher should be "a pray-er before being a speaker." Receiving before presuming to give, the preacher, before all else, must be open to God: "At the very moment he steps up to speak, before he even opens his mouth and says a word, let him lift up his thirsty soul to God, begging that it may belch forth what it has quaffed, or pour out what he has filled it with."[3] It's an image similar to Benedict XVI's aphorism, and probably where he got it: "Without prayer, preaching dries up by itself."[4] Every Christian must pray, but for the preacher especially it's an essential tool of the trade. Without prayer, it's not just that we'll end up preaching poorly, but that we'll end up preaching nothing.

Prayer is essential because it sustains wonder and openness to the mystery preachers must know, even if only partially, in order to preach the Gospel of Jesus Christ. "One can speak about God," Benedict XVI said, "only if one has not forgotten how to look, to wonder, to pause before the whole of reality, to listen to the deep foundations of being."[5] Without prayer, wonder fades, and then necessarily our preaching. This, of course, is the tragedy and the evangelical crime: that because of our lack of wonder, people may not see the wonder of the Gospel. Seeking God, they're confounded by our spiritual staleness, by the poorness of our preaching born of the poorness of our prayer.

Earlier I called for deeper intellectual life for the sake of evoking that wonder that is the beginning of the human pursuit of truth. So likewise, here my plea is that along with intellectual depth, we also renew spiritual depth, for the wonder of creation and for the wonder of the Creator. This demands prayer—simple, genuine, steadfast prayer.

Now, for the preacher, prayer will take a certain normative form, allowing, of course, for reasonable personal differences. Yet it will be a rule of life recognizably similar because of the ecclesial nature of our vocation as well as the ecclesial nature of preaching. And that's what this chapter is about: the ecclesial form of prayer shaped principally by the Liturgy of the Hours, by lectio divina, and by mental prayer, or what the *Catechism* calls "contemplative prayer."

For the preacher, the tradition is clear: prayer is more important than anything else—more than study, more than experience, more than rhetorical skill. The *Catechism* calls it "one of the secrets of the kingdom" (*CCC*, 2660), but it's one of the secrets of preaching too. Prayer separates preachers and other ministers of the Gospel from mere speakers upon the subject of Christianity, the former sustained by God himself, the latter only by personal effort. The way of the preacher must be the way of prayer, first and always.

# The Liturgy of the Hours

The first type of prayer essential to preaching is the Liturgy of the Hours, which by Church law must frame the daily prayer life of clergy.[6] It's the foundation that must first be firmly laid, becoming for bishops, priests, and deacons something habitual, even existential. Naturally, therefore, this is true for preachers. It comes before all else.

But this is often not the case. For many clergy—let's be honest—the Liturgy of the Hours can be a burden and struggle. Tucked in sideways into our busy days, the Liturgy of the Hours is often prayed in a rush, jammed in between meetings or Masses or hospital calls. Or it's put off until just before bed, when we mumble through the psalms, struggling to stay awake. For many of us, faithfully celebrating the Liturgy of the Hours is hard. Rushing through it or skipping it altogether, we sometimes feel that it hangs over us like an albatross of spiritual guilt. Some of us have probably given up on it altogether, not because of any great sin or because we're bad clergy but simply because we're busy and tired and because it's an easy thing to neglect.

However, neglecting the Liturgy of the Hours is a spiritual crisis of the first order, and for the preacher, it's deadening. And that's because the Liturgy of the Hours is like the foundation of a house; it must be well laid and firm before anything can be built on it. If it begins to crack or weaken, it must be repaired before any other damage is done, before the doors go funny and the walls begin to crack. It is, quite literally, that important, whether we realize it or not.

The Liturgy of the Hours presents an opportunity for preaching. Although not immediately obvious, the renewal of the Hours and the renewal of Catholic preaching belong together, the renewal of one leading to the renewal of the other and then to the renewal of the entire Church.

The reason we clergy often experience the Liturgy of the Hours as a burden is because we're doing it wrong. If we pray the Hours as if it's a private devotion, it makes sense that we sometimes feel it's impossible to maintain, and that we begin to dismantle it, rush through it, or ignore it. Because, individually, it *is* impossible to maintain. The Liturgy of the Hours isn't meant to be prayed the way we often pray it, by ourselves quietly and alone. By nature, it is corporate prayer meant to be prayed publicly—prayed not in clerical isolation but with others, priests and laity together.

Remember why the Church says the Liturgy of the Hours is so important, theologically and traditionally. Theologically, it is the prayer of the whole Church, offering in the voice of Christ praise addressed to the Father, prayer made possible by the presence of the Holy Spirit in the Church (see *CCC*, 1174–1175). Adopted as children of God in Christ, we pray to the Father, crying "Abba," together in Christ as sons and daughters of God (see Rom 8:15). The Liturgy of the Hours is the priestly work of the entire Body of Christ, our common address to the Father. It's the unceasing prayer of the Son that makes possible the unceasing prayer of the Church in the unceasing prayers of her saints, both on earth and in heaven (see 1 Thes 5:17). Fundamentally, that's the Liturgy of the Hours: the Son's eternal praise of the Father, offered in the voice of Christ temporally in the voice of the Church.

Eternal praise experienced in time—that's what the Liturgy of the Hours is. It's what explains the traditional division of daily prayer into certain hours of the day, a tradition first Jewish and then Christian. Just as Daniel and the Psalmist prayed at set times of the day, so too did the apostles (see Dn 6:11; Pss 55:18, 119:64). The apostles were devoted to "the prayers," as Luke reports (Acts 2:42). It's clear that included the traditional daily prayers of Jewish piety: both Peter and John still praying at certain hours of the day, good Jews that they were (see Acts 3:1; 10:9; 10:30). This is how in prayer, practically speaking, time shares in eternity; ceaseless prayer is possible by punctuating the day with set times of prayer.

For early Christians, not only was it daily prayer, but it was corporate prayer. Prayer was a corporate act before it was an individual one. That is, of course, almost exactly the opposite way we modern Christians normally think about prayer. The tradition of daily corporate prayer, the tradition behind the Liturgy of the Hours, is rooted in the theological reality of the spirit-filled Body of Christ, a reality that makes us brothers and sisters of one another as much as it makes us individual children of God. And this reality manifested itself in the way early Christians prayed—subtly different from us—more one in heart and mind than we.

Jesus gave us the Lord's Prayer, for instance, to be offered to *our* Father so that we could pray that he delivers *us* from evil (see Mt 6:7–13). No extant version of the Lord's Prayer begins "*My* Father," offered only for *me*. St. Cyprian said, "Our prayer is public and common; and when we pray, we pray not for one, but for the whole people, because we the whole people are one."[7] Early Christians saw this more clearly than we do today. From the *Didache* to Tertullian to St. Clement of Alexandria to Origen and to Cyprian, to name but a few, the evidence is clear that for early Christians, corporate prayer was not only essential—it was the norm. For them, daily prayer was "breathing together," spiritual respiration, the air of praise breathed by *all* the faithful. It's how their lives were taken up into the "single great prayer" of Christ.[8]

And it's precisely what's lacking today, especially in parish ministry: the corporate sense and, more importantly, the corporate practice of the Liturgy of the Hours. It's why the Liturgy of the Hours seems such a burden sometimes, because we treat it like a private devotion. Both the Second Vatican Council and Pope Paul VI tried to correct the privatization of this intrinsically corporate way of prayer, calling upon clergy to restore the public recitation of the Liturgy of the Hours, but unfortunately to little avail *(Sacrosanctum Concilium,* 100; *Laudis Canticum).* Divine Office books are still tucked away in private on bedside tables, and most of the lay faithful know nothing of it at all.

The Church's largely unrealized hope here, as far as I can understand it, is to restore the practice of corporate public prayer by offering the Liturgy of the Hours in parishes. Seeing it less as a private clerical duty, we should make it more genuinely a work of the people. Publicly praying the Liturgy of the Hours—daily, regularly, and at set times— would not only restore an ancient form of prayer to its proper place in the larger Body of Christ but also enliven communion and invigorate the inner spirit of the Church. Unachieved still, it remains an urgent spiritual need in the contemporary Church.

Now it's fair to wonder at this point what on earth any of this has to do with preaching. The answer is, quite a lot. As I said earlier, the renewal of the Liturgy of the Hours and the renewal of Catholic preaching go hand in hand, one leading to the other. Precisely what I mean is that the renewal of the Liturgy of the Hours—restoring it as a public office—can foster renewed preaching. No gimmicks, no programs, just this ancient form of prayer. The Liturgy of the Hours is a simple and practical first step on the road to better preaching.

And that's because the Liturgy of the Hours can help the preacher, as well as the lay faithful who join in this prayer, further cultivate the "ecclesial consciousness" Benedict XVI mentioned, forming them together as persons of the Church.[9] That is, by means of the Liturgy of the Hours, the preacher's ecclesiastical *ethos* will become less an idea and more a practice, something lived and not just thought.

The Liturgy of the Hours is the prayer of the Church, the voice of the Bride and Bridegroom offered together in praise, the Son's eternal praise of the Father refracted in time *(Sacrosanctum Concilium,* 84). But it's also an ongoing conversation with and within scripture and tradition. Praying daily with others—the psalms, readings, and hymns of the liturgical seasons of the Church's year—will slowly make a profound impact on those who experience it. As the *Catechism* says, the Liturgy of the Hours "transfigures" time, but it can also transfigure people, turning minds and hearts to God, to his will and kingdom (*CCC*, 1174).

Peter Ochs, the Jewish thinker, describes daily prayer's power to "transfigure." Writing about morning prayer from a Jewish context, he calls it "redemptive thinking." In the practice of daily prayer, he says, a person is slowly trained "to offer judgements in a different way, which means to perceive the world differently and act in it differently." When one speaks repeatedly the words of God in prayer, the effect is cognitively redemptive, introducing the person who prays to "better logics."[10]

In the Catholic context, the effect is the same. One finds this sort of redemptive thinking, for example, in John Cassian. Meditating on the phrase, "O God, make speed to save me: O Lord, make haste to help me," Cassian called it a "saving formula" that one should "not cease to chant." For him, it was a mantra fit to be said at every moment and at the beginning of every activity of the day. "When you wake," he said, "let it be the first thing to come into your mind, let it anticipate all your waking thoughts, let it when you rise from your bed send you down on your knees, and thence send you forth to all your work and business, and let it follow you all day long."[11] Cassian thought the language of daily prayer influenced behavior, not like magic but instead as habituation. Such words, much like the constant slogans of modern advertising, had the power to change thinking, desire, and behavior.

To take another example from today's Liturgy of the Hours, to say every morning, "Lord, open my lips" is, slowly but profoundly, to understand something about reality. It's to understand that God, our Creator, gives us breath and voice, that our words are not our own, but that the words we speak to God and to one another have behind them divine cause and therefore purpose. It's to understand that our speech is in some sense sacramental.

At the same time, it transfigures our conception of the universe. To say every day, "Lord, open my lips," is to form ourselves as persons in communion with God, deeply inscribing in us the truth that God *is*, and that he is not us but instead something utterly holy, *mysterium tremendum*, a Being wholly other but with whom we may still relate. That is, the Liturgy of the Hours opens the universe, revealing slowly, almost subliminally, creation, God, and his will.

It sounds astonishing to say at first, but it's true: the Liturgy of the Hours changes how we see everything, born of what the *Catechism* calls "the habit of being in the presence of the thrice-holy God" (*CCC*, 2565). Ordering our minds, our bodies, and our words toward God and the Gospel, the Liturgy of the Hours (along with the Eucharist) makes being ecclesial something existential. It makes the faith more real, more ordinary, more simply and seamlessly a part of our lives.

And this matters for preaching because there is no habit, no practice better suited to the deep preparation of homilies than the Liturgy of the Hours. There is no habitat more conducive to the preparation of homilies than the small community gathered daily around its preacher, all praying the Liturgy of the Hours, listening together to scripture, praying the psalms, speaking together the voice of the Bridegroom as the Bride—that is, as the praying Church, speaking Christ's endless praise of the Father.

Years ago, the bishops of the United States recommended that preachers create "homily preparation groups." The idea was that the preacher should gather a group of four or five people every week to go through a seven-step process of listening, reflection, and sharing, all in preparation for the next week's homily.[12] It's an idea that didn't catch on. And that's because, with all due respect, it was an artificial idea. It was just another meeting, a concocted experience. Such a meeting may be a good way to prepare for a speech, but certainly not a homily. That's because a homily is a more organic thing, born of deep, sustained prayer. By its nature, it's not the product of a meeting.

It would be better if the preacher prays the Liturgy of the Hours with people in the parish. This sort of spiritual ad hoc committee naturally makes for a far more helpful "homily preparation group," one better suited to forming the preacher within the living tradition of prayer and listening to scripture. The casual conversations, the friendships, the silences, and the rhythms of daily prayer experienced by a small community committed to praying the Liturgy of the Hours would form a preacher more deeply than any scheduled meeting or any seven-step process. It would make for better preparation.

More organic, more ascetic, more rooted in the soil of the Church's unceasing prayer, praying the Liturgy of the Hours in community would make homily preparation surprisingly less difficult, less like work. Preaching would become simply another part of the ongoing conversation of praise, experienced every day with others. Paced by the rhythm of the Church's prayer, experienced with the People of God, preaching really would become easier, more natural. Preaching would become more purely an expression of prayer, and not just the outcome of a meeting or focus group. It would be preaching that's deeper and better, born of a community gathered not by appointment but by the eternal praise of Christ to the Father.

# Lectio Divina

The second type of prayer essential to preaching is lectio divina. Recommended most notably by Pope Benedict XVI in *Verbum Domini* (sec. 8), both John Paul II and Pope Francis emphasized it as well, particularly for preachers.[13] Benedict, however, was most explicit, leaving little doubt that he thought this practice more than merely optional. "Those aspiring to the ministerial priesthood," he wrote, "are called to a profound personal relationship with God's Word, particularly in lectio divina." For him, lectio divina uniquely "nurtures" the preacher's vocation and "proper mission" (*Verbum Domini*, 82).

The Church's recent emphasis on lectio divina is due to its popular rediscovery and broad renewal in the twentieth century, thanks to people such as Jean Leclercq and Henri de Lubac. A unique form of prayer, it's born of centuries of monastic practice, of a tradition including St. Benedict and all his spiritual sons and daughters, St. Jerome and his Aventine Circle, Origen and all those wild monks and spiritual mothers of the Egyptian and Judean deserts.[14] A tradition of prayer theologically rooted in the gospels, in the necessity to hear the voice of Christ in order to live, it goes back to the word first spoken by God to his people: "Hear, O Israel!" (Dt 6:4; see Jn 5:25).

Such is the rich spiritual tradition that the Church calls us to embrace, daily and deeply: this straightforward way of prayer drawn from an immense, radiating treasury of wisdom. No gimmick, no mere method, but a much deeper, more formative practice, its depth and vibrancy are why Benedict recommended lectio divina so forcefully. "I am convinced of it," he said. He thought, if genuinely taken up, it would bring about a "new spiritual springtime" in the Church, and certainly in ministry.[15]

It also explains why Benedict outlined lectio divina in detail in his apostolic exhortation. A simple process, it begins with *lectio*—that is, simply reading—preferably aloud, as the ancients did, reenacting thereby the aural experience of hearing God's Word, an experience that's profound even now in our noisy world.[16] The point of lectio is simply to ask the question, "What does the biblical text say in itself?" (*Verbum Domini*, 87). Necessarily the first step, it helps us find God's Word and not ours, ideally keeping us from mistaking our *logos* for God's.

The next stage is *meditatio*, which in ancient practice was something akin to what we mean by memorization, but also more. In meditatio the reader allows for a sort of deep inscription of the biblical word to be cut upon his or her heart—but also upon the mind, because there is in meditatio the practice of reason.[17] It is thinking about the text, a sort of spiritual close reading that draws the audible Word of God near. Not just the Word of God in itself, in meditatio it becomes a word *for me*. In meditatio I begin to respond to the Word of God. I ask the question, "What does the biblical text say to us?" (*Verbum Domini*, 87).

This then is the beginning of prayer, *oratio*. Hearing the Word, understanding it to be God's Word and not mine, but a word nonetheless meant for me, oratio is the expression of desire that has naturally arisen in both the mind and heart, desire for God and for what he promises in the biblical Word. "What do we say to the Lord in response to his word?" is the way Benedict, perhaps too professorially, describes it (*Verbum Domini*, 87). Oratio is a form of love such as philosophers and theologians speak of, but open to every emotion any lover may experience, open to all the traumas and tantalizations of desire—but it is desire for God, the best lover. If meditatio is about mind and heart, oratio is about heart and voice, about love bold enough to speak.

Prayer, which is a form of love, is requited in the gift of *contemplatio*, the next stage of lectio divina. It is, as Benedict describes it, "a gift from God, his own way of seeing." If oratio is desiring the Lover, contemplatio is seeing the Lover, but also more. As anyone can see a woman or a man, no one sees them like his or her spouse. Likewise, no one knows a husband like his wife knows him, nor a wife like her husband. Similarly, contemplatio is not just seeing; it's seeing with a gift of knowing, which is mystically present in the soul in love with God. Like spouses, so long in love that they know each other's minds and finish each other's sentences, through contemplatio we are formed in the mind of Christ, accepting the "vision of reality, as God sees it" (*Verbum Domini*, 87).

And this inevitably changes things. Taking on the mind of Christ in contemplatio, we move on to *actio*. Benedict says actio is that "which moves the believer to make his or her life a gift for others in charity," a profounder description than one might at first think if one notices the sacrificial and eucharistic allusions at work (*Verbum Domini*, 87). Actualization of a biblical passage, the final fruit of lectio divina, is the discovery of "what the text has to say at the present time."[18] More simply and more vibrantly, it is action that follows from having taken on the "mind of Christ," action that is always love, always truth, always cruciform, and always eucharistic.

Now the reasons for lectio divina, and the reasons for Benedict passion in recommending it, are, as we can see, deeper than we might have first appreciated. The Church recommends it not as method but as transformation. The overall effect of lectio divina, as Raymond Studzinski describes it, is to participate in the ongoing creativity of God. "To appropriate lectio divina as habitual practice," he suggests, "is an act of faith in God who does still speak today; to ponder a text, reading it slowly, connects one with a God whose creative action is encountered once more."[19] Lectio divina is not about taking on any sort of "worldview," about finding mere scriptural allegories or analogies in the world; it's about taking on God's view—seeing, by means of a divine gift, the way God sees. "It is to see the more that is there," Studzinski says.[20] It is a far more inexhaustible and hopeful vision than could be got by merely mining a text for something to say on Sunday.

And so lectio divina is valuable for preachers because it not only helps them read and understand scripture but also it helps them read and understand themselves, their community, and their world from within scripture, seeing all of it enveloped within the universal story of God, Israel, and the Church. More than offering mere familiarity with scripture or the ability simply to quote passages, lectio divina forms the preacher as a *speaker* of scripture. The preacher, as Carol Harrison describes it, learns to "voice" scripture, to speak the Word of God in such a way that, through the preacher, the Word of God enters a transformative dialogue with peoples and cultures.[21]

Benedict evokes a better, more ancient image when he talks about becoming a "living exegesis" of scripture. "The most profound interpretation of scripture comes precisely from those who let themselves be shaped by the word of God through listening, reading, and assiduous meditation" (*Verbum Domini*, 48). This is, quite simply, sanctity: to become a living exegesis of the Bible—our words and deeds spoken and done creatively in harmony with God's Word, revealing thereby the proper "interpretation" of scripture (*Verbum Domini*, 83).

The idea of becoming a living exegesis evokes the desert tradition of ancient Egypt and Judea, the tradition of the *apophthegmata* or "sayings" of Desert Fathers and Mothers.[22] Many of these sayings are framed as dialogue between monks, a junior asking his elder for a "word" or some sort of advice. The elder monk always responds with some saying, sometimes explicitly biblical but often simply allusive. When Abba Poemen, for example, says, "If a person blame himself, he will be steadfast elsewhere," his "word" evokes, at least, the tax collector in Luke's gospel and maybe even Paul's warning against judging others (see Lk 18:9–14; Rom 2:1).[23] The "word" is biblical but also unique and creative, spoken by a person so saturated in scripture that he or she can't help speaking biblically.

And this, I think, is the goal of lectio divina, and why I think Benedict was so passionate recommending it to the Church. His hope was that ministers of the word and others would tap into this powerful tradition with its living spiritual energy, that they too would be able to have a "word" for spiritual seekers still wandering around this post-faith world. The point of lectio divina is far more than learning scripture, memorizing it, and drawing nearer to God in contemplation. It's to become a living form of scripture, speaking not simply about God's Word but God's Word itself.

And given the state of affairs in the Western world today, where faith and culture and even the Church have suffered debilitating crises of credibility and doubt, perhaps this is just the sort of provocative image ministers of the Word should consider and emulate: the preacher as a sort of new desert monk. So immersed in scripture and prayer, he becomes God's voice in the world, offering a "word" for those still seeking—and maybe even for those who aren't.

# Contemplative Prayer

The final type of prayer essential to preaching is what the *Catechism* calls contemplative prayer, or what is sometimes called mental prayer. Unlike the Liturgy of the Hours and even lectio divina, contemplative prayer is exclusively private and personal. Prayer of the inner room, behind closed doors, it is prayer done in secret, and it is rewarded secretly (see Mt 6:6).

Contemplative prayer, of course, is for everyone. For preachers, though, it's lifeblood. But what exactly are we talking about? And why is it important? Thomas Aquinas, faithful Dominican that he was, taught clearly that contemplation made the *vita apostolica* possible. The form of life "in which a man, by preaching and teaching, delivers to others the fruits of his contemplation" was, Thomas said, "chosen by Christ" and is therefore literally the divine model for preachers.[39]

And he taught what he lived. Asked once to speak on the Eucharist, Thomas took a little time to pray first. Kneeling before a cross, his own arms crossed, with his open notebook in front of him, he sought in prayer the truth he wanted to speak. Thomas said he wanted to consult the person he was asked to talk about, to go to the source.[25] That, very simply, is what Thomas meant by connecting contemplation and preaching—nothing heady or pretentious at all.

What Thomas taught and practiced is nothing more than what the apostles taught and practiced. It's what Jesus told Nicodemus his apostles would do: they would speak about what they know and testify to what they have seen (see Jn 3:11). The apostolic authority to preach Christ isn't built upon conjecture or "cleverly devised myths," but rather on firsthand experience, because the apostles "had been eyewitnesses of his majesty" (2 Pt 1:16). As described in the First Letter of John:

> What was from the beginning,
>     what we have heard,
>     what we have seen with our eyes,
>     what we have looked upon
>     and touched with our hands
>     concerns the Word of life—
> for the life was made visible;
>     we have seen it and testify to it
>     and proclaim to you the eternal life
>     that was with the Father and was made visible to us—
> what we have seen and heard
>     we proclaim now to you,
>     so that you too may have fellowship with us;
>     for our fellowship is with the Father
>     and with his Son, Jesus Christ. (1 Jn 1:1–3)

This is contemplation, simply and plainly. It's what the apostles experienced, as well as Thomas and innumerable others. It is the experience of Christ, of encountering him. That's contemplation, nothing more and nothing less. And it's fundamental to the preacher's life and art, and always will be.

The *Catechism* teaches that contemplation is "a *gaze* of faith, fixed on Jesus." It's prayerful attention set upon the Lord and the mysteries of his life (*CCC*, 2715). "The object of contemplation is God," Hans Urs von Balthasar said.[26] It's the sort of "seeing" that Jesus said was possible after rebirth in water and Spirit, the sort of seeing that sees in the Son of Man lifted up on the Cross the revelation of God (see Jn 3:3–5, 14–15; 8:28).

But the thing is, in contemplation, God gazes back. As Paul put it, no matter how much we know God, we are even better known by him (see 1 Cor 13:12). "LORD, you have probed me, you know me," the Psalmist wrote. "Behind and before you encircle me and rest your hand upon me. Such knowledge is too wonderful for me, far too lofty for me to reach" (Ps 139:1, 5–6). That's the difference between prayer and philosophy. To "know thyself" one must first know God and that he knows you, which is knowledge only achievable in prayer.

That's what happens in contemplative prayer. In the prayerful sharing of friendship, which is covenant and communion, a person, by a gift of grace, is slowly conformed to God (*CCC*, 2709, 2713). "God's gaze is not passive," Balthasar said; "his gaze is creative, generative, originative." Mary Magdalene's experience here is exemplary, Jesus speaking her name in the early light of Easter. "This personal name, uttered by the lips of him who is Eternal Life, is a person's true concept."[27] Beginning to see God, we discover that we are already seen by the God who created and knows us already.

But to see and hear God is also to be convicted, challenged, and changed. "When Christ calls a man, he bids him come and die."[28] That's Dietrich Bonhoeffer's famous dictum, simply restating the repeated teaching of Paul. It's a principle found across the traditions of Christianity, that in the encounter with Christ, the self is transformed, utterly.

One of my favorite illustrations of this is from an old tale about the fourth-century monk Pachomius, father of cenobitic monasticism. One evening, confronted with a vision of Christ, crisp and clear, he rejected the vision as a demonic mirage almost instantly. Even though what he saw looked so much like Christ, he said, "It is clear that he deceives me." He rejected the vision not because it wasn't convincing but because he was still conscious of self.[29]

Such is the necessary sacrifice of genuine contemplation. The person daring to begin this sort of prayer must be willing to give up the self entirely. Such a person must allow Christ to charge, try, and convict the self on every count. "If we fail to let the word's sharp edge have its effect on us, we shall always be meeting a merely imaginary Redeemer," said Balthasar.[30] In true contemplation, the fire of Christ's word burns away all the nonsense of the sinful self, searing away all that is pointless and proud. Christ's light exposes all that doesn't belong, only then revealing the true self (see Jn 3:20).

But contemplative prayer isn't navel-gazing. It's rooted always in scripture. The sort of contemplative prayer recommended in the *Catechism* leans away from those types of contemplative prayer found in the ancient traditions of the East, which seek after "formlessness," however valuable such contemplation may be. Rather, by contemplative prayer, the Church means contemplation of the scriptural Christ and the mysteries of his life. "Contemplation's ladder, reaching up to heaven," Balthasar said, "begins with the word of scripture, and whatever rung we are on, we are never beyond this hearing of the word."[31]

Now it's one of the blessings of Catholicism that there are many methods of contemplative prayer available, and here the preacher would do well to discover personally the method that works best. Given the preacher's task, however, perhaps the most accessible method of prayer is the Spiritual Exercises of St. Ignatius. By its design it is adaptable and demands the powers of imagination. A preacher wanting to practice contemplative prayer could do so profitably either by simply taking each of the four weeks in turn or by contemplating one of the mysteries of Christ's life noted near the end of the Exercises. Of course, when starting out it would be helpful to have an experienced guide, but even without, the Exercises are simple enough for anyone to use on one's own.

The reason the Exercises are so valuable, and especially for preachers, is because they invite the contemplative into the mysteries of Christ's life, enlivening the powers of imagination, powers that are elemental to good preaching. The Exercises help the preacher see the stories of the gospels from the inside out, seeing oneself in the stories to be preached. Few methods of prayer can do what the Exercises can, making the stories of scripture immediate and real. This is why, for the preacher, the Exercises offer such promise.

The Exercises facilitate true contemplation. As Ignatius wrote at the beginning of the Exercises, at the heart of them is a conversation, in which it is possible for the "Creator to deal directly with the creature, and the creature directly with his Creator and Lord."[32] That is, the Exercises help bring about the experience of Thomas Aquinas, the apostles, and all those innumerable others. They help us see and know the Lord directly, not just read about him. Benedict XVI said, "Any statement about a person one does not know is just theory, secondhand testimony."[33] That's why the knowledge gained in contemplation is essential to preaching, because our homilies must be firsthand accounts. Because it's God's Word that is preached, not just the homilist's.

The reason contemplation is necessary for the preacher is finally this: to preach meaningfully at all, the words the preacher speaks must ultimately belong not to the preacher but to Christ. The homilist must be given the words to preach. The preached word must always be Christ's word, come to the preacher from the outside by prayer. Otherwise the preacher's words are inevitably dull, lifeless, or merely dogmatic. What contemplation gives are living words born of experience. That's why contemplation is vital to preaching, because it turns the homily into a firsthand account, making it a matter of witness instead of wit.

To put it another way, the fruit of contemplation, to quote the philosopher Josef Pieper, is the *verbum cordis*, the "heart's word," an image taken from Thomas's trinitarian theology.[34] It's an image that names well the intimate and deeply personal reward of contemplation, a word born in the heart and that belongs entirely to Christ, but that the preacher still owns personally. They are Christ's words, but the homilist's words too. Only contemplation bears such fruit. It's the offspring of a soul's love and union with the Lord. And really, it's the only thing that separates a homily from a book report. It's the only thing that makes it, in truth, a homily at all: the presence of Christ's words in ours.

# The First Way of the Preacher

Remember again Phillips Brooks's definition of preaching—truth through personality. It's only prayer that makes such preaching possible. It's what allows the word of God to come "*through* the man," Brooks said, and not merely "*across* the man."[35]

Prayer is the first way of the preacher. All else done in preparation for a homily is merely an effect of prayer. Taking up the prayer of the Church in the Liturgy of the Hours, taking up lectio divina and contemplative prayer, the preacher prepares from the inside out. Better than any contrived program, these ancient forms of prayer can make preparation easier, delivery more natural, and the preacher's word more divinely as well as more humanly powerful. This can happen if we'll only gather together, get on our knees, and pray as the Church teaches us to pray, as our forebears did in ages past, in those ages of better prayer and better preaching.

# 5.

# THE WAY
# OF PREPARATION

It is only watching, waiting, attention.
—Simone Weil, *Waiting for God*, 64

Sitting under the fig tree, he doesn't realize that everything's about to change. Though it's hardly believable at first, nonsense on the face of it, he's about to see something he hadn't before. He'll never be the same. But first, he's incredulous.

"Nazareth? What good comes from Nazareth?" Nathanael's contempt isn't even thinly veiled. What good, he thinks, could ever come from that backwoods corner of Galilee?

But Philip is adamant, as much as Nathanael is unbelieving.

"We've found him!" he tells Nathanael breathlessly. "The one Moses wrote about, the prophets too. Jesus, from Nazareth!" Swept up by the charisma of this Jesus whom John had just pointed out, who gathered a few followers, and who called him to follow, Philip cares not for arguments or prejudice but for experience. "Come and see," he tells Nathanael.

But Jesus already sees Nathanael and, just after Philip, speaks to him as if he was there all along.

"Here's a true Israelite! There's no guile in him!" Jesus says, I imagine, with a wry smile, a laugh. But Nathanael is still skeptical. "How do you know me?" His is a strange experience, not spiritual at all. Really, it's downright weird.

But then there's the odd little detail, the flash of faith, light, and a word. "I saw you under the fig tree, even before Philip arrived," Jesus says.

And suddenly Nathanael sees. He speaks, and he preaches: "You are the Son of God! The king of Israel!" (see Jn 1:43–49). And everything's changed. He's not the same.

# The Preacher, Nathanael

Nathanael, I like to think, was a preacher. At least, he could have been. Exactly who he was isn't really known; the tradition isn't clear. He certainly had the stuff of a preacher. He knew how to speak truthful words, not just words—full and not empty. And he knew how to get there, how to see before he spoke.

I suspect Nathanael was a preacher because of this odd encounter told at the beginning of John's gospel, this strange exchange between him and Philip and Jesus. An experience paradigmatically homiletic, it was a providence of experiences internal and external, human and divine, which gave birth to new words and changed everything. "Rabbi, you are the Son of God; you are the King of Israel" (Jn 1:49). That was Nathanael's homily, short but perfect. Perfect, because it proclaimed and praised the Christ who was present, whom he saw and experienced himself.

But, of course, Nathanael's words aren't inexplicable or out of the blue. On the surface, it may seem that way, perhaps that he's been irrationally taken in by Jesus' charisma—maybe like the others, or maybe a bit gullible. But that's not the case. Even a brief study of the text gives clues as to what's going on, to the underlying conditions of the moment that led Nathanael to speak, when he finally saw Jesus for who he was.

Consider the scene, the interplay of characters, the allusions. Called by Jesus, Philip in turn calls Nathanael, the first evangelism. Sitting under a fig tree, that biblical symbol of messianic peace, that rabbinic symbol of the study of Torah, Nathanael—as Jesus said—is a true

Israelite, guileless.[1] Augustine assumed he was an "educated man and learned in the law," a scribe perhaps.[2] Maybe he was reading under that fig tree, scroll in hand, as Philip ran up to him.

If so, what could he have been reading? Or if he wasn't reading anything, as a learned scribe, what might he have been thinking? What coalesced in that moment, in heart and mind, that provoked his sudden faith?

Perhaps Nathanael thought of Jacob—Father Israel himself—full of guile as he was, but who, in his struggle, saw the face of God nonetheless (see Gn 27:35; 32:23–31). Perhaps, hearing where Jesus was from, Nathanael thought about *nēser*, the Hebrew root and meaning of the name "Nazareth." It means "branch" or "shoot." Perhaps that made him think of the prophecy of Isaiah about the "root of Jesse" and the rule of Immanuel (see Is 11:1–10). Or perhaps the name of Jesus caught his imagination, *Yeshua*. Maybe that made him think of Zechariah's strange, uncertain prophecy of another *Yeshua*, of the investiture of Joshua the high priest and of the coronation of that enigmatic royal figure called in the text "branch," a mysterious crowned servant, either king or priest or both (see Zec 3:1–10; 6:11). Perhaps he thought about all of this.

Maybe this was in his mind as Philip came to him, as he began to talk excitedly about Jesus from Nazareth, the one promised by Moses and the prophets. When Jesus called him guileless, a true Israelite, saying he'd seen Nathanael strangely beforehand under the fig tree, maybe that was the moment Nathanael—there in the presence of Jesus—thought about Joshua the high priest, the royal "branch," and the messianic rest under the shadow of the figs foretold by Micah (see Mi 4:4). Maybe in that revelatory moment Nathanael saw what he hadn't seen before, and so he said what he'd never said before, words that would change him forever: "Rabbi, you are the Son of God; you are the King of Israel."

Thomas Aquinas said that Nathanael was converted *per spirationes internas*, by internal inspiration or insight.[3] It's an apt description of his formation in faith, formed by witness and scripture and the presence of Christ, which all came together in a moment—seeing, speaking, and proclaiming Christ.

It's also a good way to think about preaching and how to prepare for it.

# Always Prepare

There is, of course, no one way to prepare a homily. Here, the Socratic analogy holds: it's like cooking.[4] Perfected, it's a matter of knack. That to speak well demands preparation is true for everyone, but how one prepares differs from speaker to speaker. For each preacher, habits and methods and routines are built over time upon principles and circumstances, personal quirks, discipline, and training. The preacher's unique way of preparation, personal and sometimes idiosyncratic, emerges only slowly after much trial and error, for there is no such thing as a preaching method ready right out of the box.

Still, the classical conventions and parts of rhetoric remain valuable, which preachers should still study and know. From Isocrates to Aristotle to Cicero to Quintilian, preachers should be familiar with the rhetorical traditions of the past. It is what our forebears did, baptizing pagan rhetoric for the sake of Christian preaching.[5] Basil the Great was taught by Libanius, for example, and Augustine borrowed from Cicero—even when they denied it, almost all of the early Christian preachers made use of pagan wisdom. And that's because, built upon so many enduring observations about human nature, such traditions remained useful.

And there still is value in these ancient traditions. Take Cicero's five parts of rhetoric, for example. By themselves, if so desired, a preacher could prepare homilies by thinking in order about invention, arrangement, expression, memory, and delivery, and do very well by it. In fact, it would cut out a lot of meandering in homilies, helping a preacher craft a message that is succinct and well spoken.

Since the beginning of Christian history, preachers have pondered and proffered various and practically innumerable methods for preaching, each borrowing, correcting, or improving one another. From Humbert of Romans and Alain de Lille in the Middle Ages to Fred Craddock, Eugene Lowry, and Thomas Long in our own day, each has made contributions to the *ars praedicandi* of the Gospel of Jesus Christ. Each offers something valuable for the preacher's craft, and it is from this collected wisdom that each preacher should freely choose the methods or parts of methods that personally fit.

But before I can say anything further, a chronic and common problem in Catholic preaching must be addressed. Before moving on, we must be honest about a bad habit belonging to all types of clergy from prelates to pastors to parochial vicars, and that is the lack of preparation.

We simply must prepare. Whoever we are, however long or little we've been preaching, we must prepare each and every week. Fred Craddock once wrote that some preachers are "capable of giving the impression that they were informed only five minutes ago that it was Sunday."[6] Sadly, this can be said of many Catholic preachers. Whether underestimating the significance of the homily, overestimating our speaking ability, or underestimating the amount of time other responsibilities might take, too many Catholic preachers give far too little effort to the necessarily demanding work of preparing homilies and delivering them.

If homily preparation is something done solely in our head; if we pay our homily no dedicated and undistracted thought at all throughout the week; if we just quickly jot down a few notes for an outline on Saturday evening or Sunday morning; if we've done no writing earlier than on the weekend; if we ever say to ourselves, "I've got this," or "I've preached this text before"—then we're really not doing what we were ordained to do. We're not living up to our vocation. Worse, we're sinning like the watchman spoken of by Ezekiel (see Ez 3:16–21)—unaware and unbothered by the burden of preaching, ignorant of the damage we do. And yes, it is that serious, and, yes, I do mean you, and me, and every preacher who has ever preached unprepared.

Such neglect is not what the Church expects of her preachers. As with art, so too with preaching, it's built on "theory and method."[7] As we saw earlier, Phillips Brooks put it best: "Do not be tempted by the fascination of spontaneousness. Do not be misled by any delusion of inspiration."[8] Pope Francis taught that "preaching is so important a task that a prolonged time of study, prayer, reflection, and pastoral creativity should be devoted to it" (*Evangelii Gaudium*, 145). To preach well "requires time and serious work," the US bishops have written.[9] It's not something to be squeezed in between meetings and visits or saved to the last minute or days off. Time for homily preparation should be on the calendar, respected and kept, and moved only for genuine emergencies. And again, yes, it is that serious.

But what does a "prolonged time" of preparation look like? An hour a day? Two hours? Walter Burghardt claimed he put four hours of preparation into every minute of his homily—is that sufficient?[10] One example of prolonged preparation is that of Martin Luther King Jr. Before his involvement in the civil rights movement, early in his ministry he spent fifteen hours each week preparing his sermon.

> When King entered his first pastorate in Montgomery in 1954, he spent at least fifteen hours each week in sermon preparation for Sunday morning worship. His systematic procedure usually began on Tuesday, when he began outlining ideas of what he wanted to say. On Wednesday he did necessary research and also thought of illustrative material, life situations always included. The actual writing of the discourse took place on Friday, and writing usually completed on Saturday night. By Sunday morning he had gained thorough familiarity with the sermon content.[11]

Now although this amount of time given to homily preparation isn't as intimidating as it sounds—it's really just a few hours a day—still, it's probably impossible for most Catholic clergy in parish ministry to achieve. Parish responsibilities, both administrative and pastoral, are simply too great for that sort of time to be given to homily preparation, especially for pastors. Maybe some priests could manage it, but probably not without neglecting other critical areas of ministry, because Catholic ministry is unique.

Before becoming a Catholic, as a Protestant minister I simply didn't appreciate the demands made on the average Catholic priest's time—the ministerial economies of scope and scale that are utterly unlike Protestant ministry. Multiple daily Masses, confessions, parish and school administration, funerals, hospital calls, random personal crises: the sheer volume of it all is unlike anything else in Christian ministry anywhere.

Some megachurches may be larger than even the largest Catholic parishes, but none make these sorts of daily demands on their clergy—sacramental demands requiring priests and no one else. Catholic ministry is different—invigorating and liberating, certainly, but also exhausting.

That is why when talking about homily preparation, choosing a method, I am mindful of how unreal so many methods seem. Coming either from the different planets of Protestant ministry and homiletics or from the leisured lecture rooms of seminaries, so many of the prevalent homiletic methods available today seem unworkable in workaday Catholic ministry. This is not to suggest that the various methods available aren't valuable or that they shouldn't be studied and applied. To the contrary, reading Thomas Long or Eugene Lowry or Bishop Kenneth Untener or Guerric DeBona will undoubtedly make someone a better preacher. For clergy just beginning their preaching ministry, close fidelity to these methods will instill good habits. However, most of us simply can't go back to class or hit the books like we used to. We don't have time to rethink the basics, survey the latest homiletic literature, issue surveys, or hold preparation meetings. Because, frankly, we're just too busy. It is why the renewal of Catholic preaching must take a different form.

Which brings us back to the heart and to Nathanael, the preacher. Assuming the character of the preacher is well formed—one's intellectual, collegial, and ecclesiastical *ethos*—and assuming the homilist is a person of sustained liturgical and personal prayer, then questions of which method of preparation to use should be easy to answer. Methods over time should become habits, applied almost by reflex. Work done early on in ministry, or at moments of renewal within ministry, should sustain us as we work our way through the more arid patches of the vineyard.

Preparing a homily should be like sitting at rest under a fig tree, after years of humble, quiet study. Our intellects, sharp and critical, even of the familiar, ought to be agile and alert enough to think deeply in the moments that happen to us, able to engage situations and persons around us with questions and honest dialogue. We should use words—not just of the mind or mere convention, not platitudes or bloodless generalizations, but words that are living truth. With the spiritual and rhetorical wherewithal to speak in the moment, we ought to be able to speak as Nathanael spoke, articulating Christ just as he saw him, because we suddenly realize his presence.

However we prepare for a homily, this should be our fundamental orientation, our spiritual and intellectual posture. We should remember what Thomas Long wrote, because it's a fundamental truth: "Christ is not present because we preach; we preach because Christ is present."[12] For the preacher, preparing a homily is about being in place and being prepared. Less about hermeneutical and rhetorical tricks and dance steps, it's more importantly a matter of seeing, a matter of attention. Experiencing Christ precedes preaching Christ. Only after the Spirit descended at Pentecost, and only after he and John healed the disabled man outside the Beautiful Gate, did Peter begin to preach. "Then Peter stood up," Luke writes (Acts 2:14). For the preacher, whatever one's plan or style, that's how the heart begins to find the way—by paying attention.

## Attention as Preparation

Rhetoric, before it is anything else, is a type of seeing. At least that's what Aristotle taught: that it is the ability "to see the available means for persuasion." Rhetoric is the ability to see the *pisteis*—that is, the proofs, the demonstrations—that compose the *logoi*—that is, the arguments of a speech.[13] Simply put, rhetoric is the capacity to see well before speaking well. This is why a good way to think of homily preparation is as seeing.

It's what Nathanael was doing, sitting under the fig tree. Seeing Philip, confronted by the passion of his witness, Nathanael saw scripture and then he saw Christ. He saw all of it in a moment, and not just with physical eyes but also with that sort of seeing called sometimes in John's gospel *theōrein*.[14] It's the sort of seeing that leads to eternal life, seeing the glory the Father gave the Son (see Jn 6:40; 17:24). It's seeing that goes beyond the material, beyond the historical and analytic. Seeing born of prayer, it is contemplative, what the *Catechism* calls the "*gaze* of faith" (*CCC*, 2715). Simone Weil called it "attention," a sort of seeing all things at once:

> Attention consists of suspending our thought, leaving it detached, empty, and ready to be penetrated by the object; it means holding in our minds, within reach of this thought, but on a lower level and not in contact with it, the diverse knowledge we have acquired which we are forced to make use of. Our thought should be in relation to all particular and already formulated thoughts, as a man on a mountain who, as he looks forward, sees also below him, without actually looking at them, a great many forests and plains. Above all our thought should be empty, waiting, not seeking anything, but ready to receive in its naked truth the object that is to penetrate it.[15]

This is the sort of seeing that belongs to homily preparation, however one goes about it. "We do not obtain the most precious gifts by going in search of them" she said, "but by waiting for them."[16] No matter the effort or the hours we put into our homilies, this open passivity remains essential. A manifold attention, it's about putting oneself in place to experience the real presence of Christ—just as Nathanael saw him, as well the centurion at the foot of the Cross and Mary Magdalene that first early Easter morning. It's about being ready when the penny drops, about finally seeing Christ in the midst of the community and pointing in praise.

But attention is often difficult to achieve in today's busy, digital, distracted world. This sort of seeing demanded of preachers is uncharacteristic of modernity. Romano Guardini, meditating almost a century ago, saw well how differently modern attention is shaped and focused, away from mystery. "Our attention today is claimed for rational and utilitarian tasks in such a way that we no longer pay attention to that other dimension of our existence." Less focused on "our innermost life" and on our natural world, our capacity to see more meaningfully the world around us—and not only what is merely material—has diminished.[17] Guardini's hope, at the dawn of the modern age, was that people would hold on to religious imagination and not foolishly throw it away. This is just the sort of seeing, the attention, that belongs to the practice of preaching. It's what is required of the homilist in preparation and delivery, and really at every stage of homiletics because the quality of our speech is always determined by the quality of our sight.

But what is there to see? In preparing a homily, there are four essential areas that demand the preacher's attention: *attention to sacred texts*, *attention to liturgy and liturgical time*, *attention to the world and to people*, and finally *attention to oneself and one's vocation*. For homilies of any sort, tending to each of these areas is critical. Woven together in study and prayer, they enable the preacher to see the living Christ and to hear the *viva vox*, the living voice of the Church. Before the preacher writes anything, before speaking, practicing this manifold attention is necessary. For it will help the homilist preach the living Christ and not the self.

## Attention to Sacred Texts

Not surprisingly, *attention to sacred texts* comes first. All preaching, to quote the well-known conciliar decree, is to be "nourished and ruled by sacred Scripture" (*Dei Verbum*, 21). But what does that mean in practice? How do preachers ensure that their preaching is genuinely scriptural, nourished and ruled by the Bible?

To begin with the obvious, paying attention to sacred texts means getting to know the biblical texts appointed for the liturgy, becoming familiar with each passage, learning about them, each in turn. But it's not just about reading the assigned passages and gathering information. Thomas Long said it's "much like getting to know another person in a profound way."[18] It's an encounter with a person and not just some ancient dead text.

And so, like meeting a new person, it's best to begin by introducing oneself. When meeting someone for the first time, it's normal to shake hands, say hello, and say your name. It's awkward and creepy to *begin* a conversation asking all sorts of probing questions about medical history or personal background. Friendships don't begin that way. Instead, they begin causally, often informally, which is a good way to begin one's relationship with Christ in scripture.

It's best to approach the texts appointed with as clear a mind as possible, momentarily putting aside, as much as one can, everything else going on in one's head—the latest book read, parish matters, politics, personal matters, and so on—and just listen to the texts as bare words. Or, as Paul Ricoeur put it, we should approach the texts naively.[19] And I mean *listen*. It's best to read the passages slowly and out loud because that's a good way to keep unwanted mental distractions at bay, and because there's something powerful about the unvarnished aural experience of scripture. Often, insights come during this first reading, graced clues nudging the preacher on to further reflection. And as with many friendships, they get better with time, so the earlier a preacher engages the sacred texts, the better.

What follows, then, is prayer—more intentional prayer, lectio divina—and then, from that, whatever formal study seems necessary. By this point, it's appropriate to have made a choice about which text or texts of the lectionary you want to "preach on," focusing prayer and study on them. It's not necessary, nor is it good stewardship of time, to contemplate and interpret every verse of every passage appointed every Sunday. Rather, trusting in one's education and in the guidance of the Holy Spirit, even this early in the process, the homilist can feel sure that the choices made at this stage are good ones, and that the texts one feels called to explore may be a matter of providence.

Thomas Long argues that a preacher shouldn't rush too quickly to commentaries at this point, but instead spend time exploring the biblical text, asking of it basic questions, jotting them down. For example, how does the passage fit within its larger context—the gospel, book, or letter from which it's taken? Is this passage a parable, poetry, prophecy, history, or a vision? Are there any allusions you can discern, any references to other themes or parts of the Bible? The preacher should be able to come about all this by closely attending to the text, drawing from one's presumably adequate familiarity with scripture—that is, if the preacher possesses a basic seminary education and a habit of reading the Bible, which, of course, a Catholic homilist should.

From this come the questions meant for the commentaries. The preacher should know how to use commentaries efficiently. General knowledge of scripture as well as amateur familiarity with the basics of biblical studies should be able to prevent the homilist from getting distracted, bogged down, or led astray by commentaries. One should always make use of good commentaries, but not waste too much time with them. Expository preaching really isn't part of the Catholic tradition, so chasing down the significance of the aorist tense of some verb in all the manuscript variants currently extant is probably a waste of a preacher's time.

The goal of biblical study and prayer, when done for the sake of preaching, is to discover the "central contribution" of each text, what Thomas Long calls the "claim of the text." The goal is exegesis, not eisegesis, which is why commentaries remain an essential part of homily preparation. Long describes the claim of the text as "a voice heard, a textual will," because, again, it's like meeting a person.[20] Essential to any good conversation is understanding, as clearly as possible, what the other person is saying. And so commentaries matter, because although encountering Christ in scripture is indeed personal, biblical interpretation nonetheless remains an encounter with a translation of a variant of ancient texts, written in foreign languages, which few mortals can decipher unaided.

For Catholic preachers, however, there's more to it than that. Paying attention to sacred texts means paying attention not only to the literal sense of scripture but also to its spiritual sense and understanding that the two always belong together.

That's what Benedict XVI sought to remind the Church in *Verbum Domini*, when, granting the proper place of philological and historical studies, he still insisted that "the letter needs to be transcended" (*Verbum Domini*, 37–35). Following theologians such as Henri de Lubac and other recoveries of patristic and theological exegesis, Benedict XVI reminded theologians and preachers that it is indeed acceptable, if not plainly necessary, to read scripture according to the classic four senses—the quadriga of the *literal sense*, the *allegorical sense*, the *moral sense*, and *anagogical sense* (see *CCC*, 115–119).

But what does that mean? Without getting lost in theological weeds, as an example, let's look at the Old Testament reading from the Second Sunday of Lent in Year A, from Genesis:

> The LORD said to Abram: Go forth from your land, your rel-
> atives, and from your father's house to a land that I will show
> you. I will make of you a great nation, and I will bless you;
> I will make your name great, so that you will be a blessing. I
> will bless those who bless you and curse those who curse you.
> All the families of the earth will find blessing in you.
>
> Abram went as the LORD directed him, and Lot went with
> him. Abram was seventy-five years old when he left Haran.
> (Gn 12:1–4)

Now, how might this text be read according to the classic four senses? First, one would want to learn the larger *literal* story of Genesis,
the mythology of earlier chapters, and the stories of Sarai and the
Egyptians, of Lot, of Hagar and Ishmael, and then of Isaac and his
descendants. But then the preacher would want to look at the passage
*allegorically*—that is, as a figure of God's ultimate plan for all his Church,
that she too may "go forth" into the Promised Land, the final Jerusalem—seeing the passage in that sense as an allegory of the Paschal Mystery. *Morally*, the passage speaks of Abram the sojourner, exemplifying
that essential element of faith: that it's a life of pilgrimage. This leaves
us to think of the passage's *anagogical sense*, seeing all the "families of the
earth" gathered finally together in John's "vision of a great multitude,
which no one could count, from every nation, race, people, and tongue,"
all standing before the Lamb (Rv 7:9).

Reading scripture this way undoubtedly adds not only depth but also
genuinely greater meaning, bringing about what Henri de Lubac called
the *Mysterium Christi*.[21] If paying attention to sacred texts is like getting to
know someone deeply, then to know scripture well, more than a study of
the literal sense is necessary. To understand a text genuinely, one must
pay attention to not only history but also spirit. "Only against this hori-
zon can we recognize that the word of God is living and addressed to
each of us in the here and now of our lives" (*Verbum Domini*, 37). That's
why, after introducing oneself to the biblical text, and after prayer and
study, one should still explore a text's classic four senses. Because often
it's what finally opens the door to understanding, which leads to seeing
the living and present eternal God.

## Attention to Liturgy and Liturgical Time

Still, the preacher is far from done. One must also pay *attention to liturgy and liturgical time*. The teaching of the Church is clear that the homily is "part of the liturgy itself" (*Sacrosanctum Concilium*, 52). This bears on the form and delivery of the homily, which we'll explore in a later chapter. First, however, it's important to grasp on a deeper level what the liturgy is in its essence and what it means for preaching.

As one draws upon scripture for a homily, so too may one draw upon "liturgical sources," not only liturgical texts but also ritual gestures and symbols (*Saccrosanctum Concilium*, 35.2). The liturgies of the Church, filled with biblical allusions, belong to the homilist's source material. Preaching on the Ascension, for example, Augustine sometimes made use of the liturgical phrase "Lift up your heart" as a way to tie Christ's ascent to the Father to the spiritual event of the liturgy.[22] Connections creatively and seamlessly made between both sacred and liturgical texts and symbols enliven the kerygma of the Gospel, bringing biblical texts to bear on the action of the liturgy itself, and in turn more closely on the lives of the faithful participating in the liturgy.

Say, for example, at Pentecost or Epiphany, or even at Christmas when extended families come together, preaching on the phrase from Eucharistic Prayer III—"gather to yourself all your children scattered throughout the world"—resonates with readings from Acts 2, Matthew 2, or Luke 2.[23] All of them are stories involving people gathering around Christ, echoing themes found in each of these liturgies. Woven together well in a homily, this phrase from the liturgy can bring about an experience, culminating sacramentally, of God's continuing action in the present, not just the past. Preached well, it can help people see God at work in their lives today, still gathering us.

But to make these connections seamlessly, and not awkwardly cut and pasted, the preacher's attention to liturgy must go even deeper, grasping the liturgy in its theological essence. The homilist must see the liturgy fundamentally as an encounter with the person and Passion of Christ.

It's how the Church wants us to see the liturgy, as set out at the very beginning of *Sacrosanctum Concilium*. The liturgy, Council Fathers taught, is that through which the "work of our redemption is accomplished," the bringing together in justice and mercy God and creation. It is an incarnate mystery, building up the faithful into a "holy temple of the Lord" in which the Spirit dwells, so that we might be made visible as the Church to "preach Christ" to the rest of the world (*Sacrosanctum Concilium*, 2). And as mystery, it's more than merely indicative. The liturgy doesn't merely signify redemption or memorialize it, but belongs to its achievement. In the liturgy, Christ, startlingly contemporary, "continues the work of our redemption" (*CCC*, 1069).

And that is true for two simple but profound reasons. First, in the liturgy, we encounter the person of Christ, who is "always present in his Church, especially in her liturgical celebrations" (*Sacrosanctum Concilium*, 7). In the sacraments of the liturgy especially, "Christ now lives and acts in and with his Church" (*CCC*, 1076). And Christ's sacramental actions are redemptive because of the Passion of Christ, which is the other great mystery encountered in the liturgy of the Church. By the Paschal Mystery, Christ is the "Mediator between God and man," reconciliation *in himself*, and the "fullness of divine worship" (*Sacrosanctum Concilium*, 5). This is why the Church says such profound things about the liturgy, because she believes that in it—as John Paul II wrote once, by a "mysterious 'oneness in time'"—we're made contemporaries of Christ and his Passion (*Ecclesia de Eucharistia*, 5). This is precisely what the preacher must see while preparing a homily, making the liturgy an object of attention.

All preaching must disclose the person and Passion of Christ. This is what the Church means when she teaches that the homily is part of the liturgy. The homily is part of the liturgy not because of its location in the Mass but because "the liturgy is the privileged setting in which God speaks to us in the midst of our lives" (*Verbum Domini*, 52). The liturgy is where we experience the living Christ, and where he speaks to us, and so the homily must always serve that liturgical miracle, the disclosure of the person and Passion of Christ. The homily is never merely words offered about an inert Gospel but instead always shares in the event of revelation. Like Nathanael under the shadow of figs, we speak because we have encountered Christ.

But essential also is attention to liturgical time, because it brings together the words of biblical and liturgical texts not only in worship but also in the lives of worshippers. Liturgical time is just that—*time*—and as such it is experienced in the present. To experience either history or the future is to experience it in the present, and so liturgical time presents a unique and indeed mysterious experience of past, present, and future in Christ within ourselves. This basic reality about time and liturgy makes it possible to hear the living Christ speak from within the mysteries that the liturgy celebrates at any point on the Church's calendar. Geoffrey Wainwright called this the "hermeneutical continuum," by which he meant simply that the liturgy is the normal context for the interpretation of scripture—that it's within liturgical time and themes that scripture is properly understood, bridging what he called the "historico-cultural gap."[24] Or to put it more plainly, the liturgy is what makes God's ancient Word new, repeatedly over millennia.

Take, for example, the readings and liturgical texts appointed for the Sundays of Advent from any of the three years of the Sunday cycle. In succession, they prepare worshippers to celebrate Christmas not only historically but also interiorly. Not only do the Advent liturgies point to the mystery of Christ's Incarnation on earth, but they point to the experience of the believing Christian's encounter with Christ. In the first week of Advent, the message is to watch; in the second week, the message is to repent and prepare; the third is to rejoice; and the fourth is to say yes to the coming of Christ. Followed as a thread, these liturgies prepare worshippers for an encounter with Christ that changes us, heals us, fills us with God's presence, and redeems us by uniting us to Christ, all of which is a type of birth.

Or consider again the reading from Genesis 12 from the Second Sunday of Lent in Year A. Falling between the Rite of Election and the First Scrutiny in the RCIA, both the biblical and liturgical texts for the day are given to a sense of journey, sacrifice, and promise. Just as Abram is commanded to "go forth" toward an unknown land, so also may catechumens feel a sense of being on a divinely driven journey from the Rite of Election through the Scrutinies on toward Holy Week and the Easter Vigil. Even without catechumens in the congregation, this sense of spiritual journey easily resonates. Like Abram, ahead of the catechumens is the Promised Land, which for them is full communion in the Catholic Church, and ultimately salvation and heaven joined together with all the faithful. But ahead of them is also sanctification, which can be linked to a meditation on the Transfiguration of Jesus in Matthew's gospel and on the grace given us in the "appearing" of Christ spoken of by Paul in the second reading from 2 Timothy. The themes of promise and destiny present in both the liturgy and lectionary possess an intrinsic momentum. And they're themes that invite discussion about the cost of the journey, the sacrifices that may be demanded of the catechumens.

Abram's leaving his comfortable surroundings behind and his willingness to sacrifice all that was dearest to him, even his son Isaac—which we recall in Eucharistic Prayers I and IV—all point to the sacrifice of the Lamb at Calvary and in the Eucharist. These speak of a God whom we seek and for whom we struggle, but who ultimately meets us where we are and gives us grace sufficient to complete our journey. Put all together, it's a word of encouragement to keep going for those still on the journey—as Peter, James, and John did, following Jesus the rest of the way to Jerusalem, to death and resurrection.

Now what brings all these varied allegories close, what makes them matters of experience, is liturgical time. The journey and sacrifice of Abraham and the journey and sacrifice of Jesus narrate our journeys—from Epiphany to Lent to Easter, from election to baptism, from old life to new life, from this world to the next. Attention to liturgical time brings the words of liturgy and scripture to bear in a profoundly personal way, more than if someone merely taught the meaning of biblical texts. This is exactly why the preacher should take note of liturgical time, because, as Benedict XVI taught, it's often in the homily that such meaning is disclosed, "bringing the scriptural message to life in a way that helps the faithful realize that God's word is present in their everyday lives" (*Verbum Domini*, 59). Often it's precisely the preacher who makes these connections.

## Attention to the World and to People

The preacher, however, isn't done paying attention. Seeing Christ, whom the homilist must proclaim and praise in the present moment, also demands *attention to the world and to people*. Pope Francis taught that a preacher should "keep his ear to the people to discover what the faithful need to hear" (*Evangelii Gaudium*, 154). Resisting the temptation to abuse the pulpit by using it as a forum for personal pet issues or for putting one's alleged expertise on display, a good preacher should be able to put the pastoral needs of the congregation above the self. That is, what a preacher wants to say and what needs to be said should be the same.

Preaching, as is all rhetoric, is a form of communication. It implies dialogue, which further implies regard for others either as interlocutors or as audience. Good rhetoric of any sort demands understanding one's audience, including where they're coming from and what they've been through. As Aristotle said, "Rhetoric is a combination of analytical knowledge and knowledge of characters."[25] It's why so much of his work *On Rhetoric* deals with *pathos* and human emotions, with things such as anger and enmity, friendliness, fear, and pity.

Since the beginning, the best Christian preachers understood this instinctively. Paul, preaching in Athens, talked about the altar of the "Unknown God" and quoted pagan wisdom (see Acts 17:23–28). In Jerusalem—knowing he was speaking to both Pharisees and Sadducees—Paul divided the Sanhedrin to his advantage by simply mentioning the "resurrection of the dead" (Acts 23:6). Paul, who became "all things to all," grasped deeply the significance and power of *pathos* (1 Cor 9:22). At its best from Christ to Paul to Pope Francis, Christian preaching demands attention to the world and to the diversity of its people, globally and locally. It demands, to again quote Gregory the Great, that the preacher "touch the hearts of his hearers by using one and the same doctrine, but not by giving to all one and the same exhortation."[26]

To pay attention to the world and to people also means paying attention to outside and opposing views, doubts and criticisms of the Gospel, of the Church and her teachings, and of our own ministry. As Benedict XVI taught, good preaching is addressed to those both inside and outside the assembly of the Church; it is alert to the half-open, half-developed hearts of some, or many, in the pews, and not just the ardent faithful.[27] It's not so much that we preachers should prepare for a visiting contingent of atheists each Sunday but that we should understand the struggles of faith that even many of the faithful endure. Aristotle taught that a good speaker, of whatever form of rhetoric, "should be able to argue persuasively on either side of a question," not so a speaker may legitimize falsehood or injustice, of course, but to make one's own argument better by treating the best opposing arguments.[28] For the preacher, this means being willing and able to take the Gospel's most pointed criticisms seriously, as well as people's sometimes visceral doubts and struggles. The preacher should resist the temptation to preach against cartoonish characterizations and straw-man arguments, but rather take people's questions and wounds thoughtfully and respectfully.

Consider the Third Sunday of Advent, Gaudete Sunday, December 16, 2012. Liturgically a day of joy, it fell two days after the tragedy of Sandy Hook, one of the most horrific mass shootings in US history, killing twenty-six innocent people, mostly six- and seven-year-old children.

My experience that weekend was probably like a lot of other preachers. The tragedy occurred on a Friday, which suddenly made the little discourse on joy I had written for Sunday—riddled with quotes from theologians and philosophers—inadequate, to say the least. Clearly I had to say something else. Sticking with what I had prepared, preaching as if Sandy Hook hadn't happened, would have been pastorally stupid and cruel. The world had dealt everyone a bitter blow that week. And so, from the Church, the people coming to Mass that Sunday needed the Gospel's comfort and hope, words of shared grief and hope of healing.

The theme that Sunday was joy, but I had to be careful how I dared talk about it. Trite, pedantic words about joy, mere exegesis or liturgical commentary, wouldn't cut it. I had to pay attention to the people and to their wounds. So, scribbling away on Saturday afternoon, I wrote an entirely different homily. My original text began with a profoundly lame question: "What is joy?" Realizing how hollow my entire original homily sounded, I decided to trade all my bright theologians for Big Bird and the wisdom of *Sesame Street*. Paying attention to the world and my congregation, I made my new homily something completely different:

> Big Bird wanted to share some pictures he had drawn of all the adults on Sesame Street—Maria, Susan, Gordon, Bob. He had worked so hard on them. They really were beautiful. The last picture he held up was of Mr. Hooper. "Ta-da!" said Big Bird. No one said a word. "I can't wait till he sees it," Big Bird said, looking into Hooper's Store, everyone still silent, looking at each other, anxious. Bob, finally, steps forward quietly,
>
> "Uh, Big Bird, he's . . . he's not in there."
>
> "Oh, then where is he?" Big Bird asks playfully.
>
> "Big Bird, uh, don't you remember," Maria says, drawing close, "don't you remember, we told you? Mr. Hooper died. He . . . he's dead."
>
> "Oh, yeah," Big Bird answers. "Well, I'll give it to him when he comes back."
>
> "Big Bird, Mr. Hooper's not coming back," Susan says gently.
>
> "Why not?"
>
> "Big Bird, when . . . when people die, they don't come back."
>
> "Ever?"
>
> "No, never."
>
> "Well, why not?" Big Bird is confused, quiet. He sighs a little—gently, sadly.
>
> Olivia wraps her arms around Big Bird. "We'll still have our memories of him," she says.
>
> "Well, yeah . . . yeah, our memories," Big Bird says slowly. "Right . . . we can remember him and remember him and remember him as much as we want to! . . . But I don't like it. It makes me sad. He's never coming back?"
>
> "No," Olivia says gently.
>
> "Well, I don't understand! You know, everything was just fine! I mean, why does it have to be this way? Give me one good reason!"
>
> "Just because," Gordon says.

"Oh."[29]

Such pure and infant confusion—it betrays the primal innocence which so convicts us in these tender days, following such a horrific shooting. "But I don't like it. It makes me sad," a child's words, a child's search for meaning—words which for their innocence all the more condemn the crime, and condemn us, we hardened makers of this world.

We should hear the voices of these children. "But I don't like it. It makes me sad." May they speak to us. May their questions, innocent and pure, show us how wicked we've made things. Let the pundits, the allegedly wise and confident, and the Facebookers be silent. Let the children speak, and we'll hear in them the sadness of God.

Now why begin a homily by narrating one of the saddest and most moving (and brilliant) scenes in the history of *Sesame Street*, where Big Bird finally learns that Mr. Hooper isn't coming back? The answer is *pathos*.

Knowing that most, if not all, of the congregation would still be reeling from a national tragedy in which twenty young children had been killed, I knew I needed to allow listeners the freedom to experience innocence and tragedy together. Knowing I should neither provide nor encourage shallow theodicies of explanation, of why God would let such horrible things happen, I sensed that Big Bird's questions, his beautiful childish anguish, would be enough to help listeners quietly articulate their own grief. "But I don't like it. It makes me sad," and, "Give me one good reason!" and his gentle, resigned "Oh"—I'm fairly sure these words allowed everyone to experience with Big Bird the sadness most were feeling just two days after Sandy Hook.

Still, neither scripture nor the liturgy were discarded. Only if utterly unworkable should the appointed readings be put to the side. Now that Sunday I didn't offer any sort of deep exegesis; rather, I took the question "What then should we do?" from Luke's gospel as a lead in to a talk about the solidarity of prayer offered for victims and for one another. John the Baptist called for acts of charity that would bind people together. After Sandy Hook, the answer to the question "What then should we do?" was to share one another's grief in prayer, believing that even such a small thing as that was a tangible and productive act of charity, a way to bind ourselves with victims and their families. Quoting Mr. Rogers—"When your heart can cry another's sadness, / Then your heart is full of love"—I invited listeners into a communion of sadness and love, suggesting that all they needed to do to be faithful in that moment was to grieve and love.[30]

Only then, really, could joy be addressed and the hope of the Church's Advent liturgy be named. Only after all this pastoral homiletic work could I finish with some glimpse of the coming Christmas:

> Today is Gaudete Sunday. "Rejoice," the Church bids us. Frankly, it's hard to rejoice today. Today we can only rejoice by faith. "The light shines in the darkness, and the darkness has not overcome it." This is our faith. May we rejoice in this today, even though it's hard. Let us rejoice by faith because the Lamb has guided them—these beautiful children—to springs of living water, and he has wiped away every tear from their eyes.

I share my experience of this homily because it illustrates what's meant by calling the preacher a "mediator of meaning," a person able to give voice to a community's concerns, name its demons, and thus "gain some understanding and control of the evil which afflicts it."[31] It shows why paying attention to the world and to people is important, and why it's as fundamental to the preacher's task as paying attention to sacred texts, liturgy, and liturgical time.

Nathanael only saw Jesus after talking to Philip. Who knows if he'd have seen him otherwise? I doubt it. Scriptural exegesis alone is not sufficient, nor is mere liturgical understanding. Rather, to see and speak the contemporary and living Christ, the homilist must pay attention, globally and locally, to the world and to people, sensitive not only to those the preacher knows and serves, but to *all* people. That is, the preacher must be attuned to *pathos*, because that too belongs to the disclosure of the living, contemporary Christ. To see Christ, the preacher must see people with eyes of love and empathy. The preacher must know the world if the world is to know Christ.

## Attention to Oneself and One's Vocation

But finally, one must pay *attention to oneself and one's vocation*. That Christian preaching always requires a preacher, that a person is involved, is so obvious that one could miss the importance of it. One might miss the significance of the fact that all the grace, insight, and truth found in the words "Rabbi, you are the Son of God; you are the king of Israel" did not sound without medium, but rather converged first upon a single person (Jn 1:49). That the homiletic event took place first *in* Nathanael, before his words were ever graced, is an important fact worthy of reflection. The fact that God would ever use such a human, fallible medium is worthy of wonder—as well as the fact that God ever used humans to speak his words, and that he still does.

This is why, after paying attention to all else, one must return to oneself, one's heart, and, as Pope Francis wrote, personalize the Word of God, allowing it to become "incarnate" in daily life (*Evangelii Gaudium*, 149–150). If preaching begins in the heart, if it's a matter of delivering "truth through personality," then paying attention to oneself should be part of every homily's preparation.[32]

It's a matter of integrity. As Fred Craddock wrote, "Appropriation of the gospel is the minimum condition for approaching the pulpit or podium." "There is something nonsensical," he said, "about the truth in the mouth of one whose life has no evidence of participation in that truth."[33] The life of the preacher, Augustine said, should "itself be a kind of eloquent sermon."[34] From beginning to end, it is the homilist who is the personal medium of the words of the preached Gospel.

The preacher must beware of romanticism here, the delusion of seeing oneself as some sort of unique saint like Chrysostom or the Curé d'Ars, too quickly and without merit. Before nodding one's head in recognition at all this talk about integrity, the preacher should remember that paying attention to oneself isn't a matter of self-congratulation, but instead it's about self-examination. As St. Benedict warned, "Do not aspire to be called holy before you really are."[35] Paying attention to oneself may first be painful, and rightly so.

Thus, once the preacher has come up with something to say, a few probing questions are in order: "How has my mind changed?"

"What new truth have I discovered preparing for this particular homily?" "Where have I been wrong?" "How should I change?" Nathanael changed his mind about Nazareth and likely about everything he thought he knew about the prophecies relating to the Messiah, all in the moment in which he found himself in front of Jesus. *Metanoia* belongs to the way of the preacher. And so, if after self-examination one doesn't occasionally find evidence of personal enlightenment and change, a preacher should be concerned that the Gospel preached may not be Christ's but instead the gospel of the self. Without *metanoia* the preacher runs the risk of preaching an anti-gospel, a false message dictated not by the truth of Christ but by the lesser motives of the world, be they personal interests, privileges, or political agendas.

The preacher should question personal fears. "How do you know me?" Nathanael asked Jesus (Jn 1:48). A question fraught with earthly fear, I imagine it was that nervous sort of fear that often precedes awe of the holy. Clearly, the Gospel is demanding, and clearly preachers are saints in progress, just like everyone else. Thus, preparing every homily, the preacher should be open to the "scrutiny of one's own spiritual life."[36] One must acknowledge earthly fears before daring to preach the fear of God.

For instance, serving in a wealthy parish, preaching about love and service to the poor, a homilist should be honest about the fear of losing popularity and maybe even pledges. It doesn't take long for a pastor to think about salaries and light bills and assessments and mortgages while preparing a homily. Anyone who's ever preached Luke's gospel, for example, knows exactly this fear. We should be candid about our fear, otherwise fear will control and ultimately ruin our preaching, no matter how materially successful such preaching may be. When we're called to preach on those more socially awkward matters of holiness, things such as sexual morality or the witness of the family, we should be honest about fears that someone might walk out angry, email the bishop, express their disappointment in us, or call us a hypocrite.

Fear casts shadows over the Gospel. But it's the preacher's task to bring the full Gospel to light, first by being honest about the shadows that personal fear casts. Honest self-examination is critical with every homily. "When writing of oneself one should show no mercy," the parish priest of Ambricourt writes in Georges Bernanos's *The Diary of a Country Priest*.[37] It's the sort of candor preachers ought to have when preparing to preach, so that they may keep from hiding from the truth that God may be giving them to speak. Such brutal honesty is necessary if the homilist is to be a preacher of truth and if the preacher is to grow in truth.

Here a little history illustrates the sort of self-attention I mean. In the middle of April 1963, Martin Luther King Jr. sat in jail in Birmingham, Alabama. There had been protests in the city for a week, but King had only recently been arrested. In his cell, opening the newspaper, he read an open letter titled "A Call for Unity," written by eight white Alabama clergymen, Protestant and Catholic. They criticized King and the protests he brought to Birmingham, calling them "unwise and untimely." A public and pointed rebuke, it must have gotten under his skin, because in response King penned one of the most hallowed texts in American history, the "Letter from a Birmingham Jail."[38] That letter, calling out white clergy who "stand on the sideline and mouth pious irrelevancies and sanctimonious trivialities," moved the conscience of a nation. But it was first written to "my dear fellow clergymen," particularly those eight men who had written "A Call for Unity."[39]

Not all the signatories of "A Call to Unity" were changed by King's letter, though; only a few. Most faded from history. Earl Stallings, however, did change. He was the pastor of First Baptist Church, and before King had even come to town, he had showed signs of both welcome and hesitation. Just a few weeks after King's letter was published, however, he preached a sermon about Pontius Pilate's indifference to Christ because he "wanted nothing to upset his little kingdom." Obviously convicted, Stallings asked his congregation, "Are we any different?"[40] He was changed and so too was his preaching. Open to *metanoia*, he preached something new.

The Catholic signatory Joseph Durick, then auxiliary bishop of Mobile–Birmingham, also changed. King's "soft words were painful to me," he said, wounding him deeply. Seeing his early reticence for what it was, he repented and lived out the rest of his ministry bravely as sometimes an unpopular voice for civil rights. He even marched with King in Memphis in 1968 and read portions of King's letter at the memorial Mass he celebrated after his assassination.[41]

Attention to oneself and one's vocation, embracing the candid habit of self-examination, being open to change and conversion—that's what these two preachers exemplified, and that's the lesson here. For Pastor Stallings and Bishop Durick, knowledge of scripture wasn't the issue, nor was knowledge of liturgy or the world. King was jailed on Good Friday, something no one could fail to notice. And they were ministers clearly bothered by what they saw going on in their city. Yet it wasn't until they allowed themselves to be convicted and changed that they finally understood the scripture they had studied. Only after their own experience of *metanoia* were they finally able to recognize Christ at work in their midst. That's what made their preaching finally Christian: that the Gospel had at last changed them.

# More Than a Skill

Paying attention: whatever the mechanics of preparation, that's what matters. Paying attention to scripture, to liturgy and liturgical time, to the world and to people, and to the self: that's what Nathanael did underneath the fig tree. And that's what we preachers must do if we, like him, are to point to Christ in proclamation and praise. More than what we preachers have learned, more than skill, what matters most is that we are able to see the Christ who is always present, standing very close, seeing us.

# 6.
# THE WAY
# OF SPEAKING

> Wisdom without eloquence does too little.
> —Cicero, *On Invention* 1.1

Seeing isn't everything. It remains for the preacher to speak. The preacher is not a visionary but a messenger. The Word of God is meant to become matter in soundwaves and synapses, in ears and brains and hearts. It's why the preacher must tend to the art of speech, its forms and methods. For the same reason that the priest can't just look at bread and wine on the altar but also must speak words to make them flesh and blood, so too it is necessary for the preacher to use words to render the Gospel real in listeners' hearts. God has given speech creative and re-creative power, ever since he spoke light into being, ever since Christ. Words are the matter of all the preacher's forms.

Our discussion thus far has concerned what the rhetorical tradition calls "invention," what Aristotle simply called *dianoia*, "the thought."[1] Tending to *ethos*, *pathos*, and *logos*, we've sketched the way the preacher first sees what to say, by paying attention to sacred texts, liturgical and human contexts, and the self. In Thomas Long's helpful terms, we've been talking about a homily's focus and function—that is, what a homily is about and what it's meant to accomplish.[2] In Phillips Brooks's words, we've discussed preaching as delivering truth through personality.[3]

But, of course, there's more to it than that. What remains is to work out exactly how to say what the homilist sees. As Aristotle said, "It is not enough to have a supply of things to say but it is also necessary to say it in the right way."[4] Peter's vision at Joppa, for instance, of all the hitherto unclean animals he was now meant to eat, and his experience in the house of Cornelius: it all had to be explained, preached carefully, step by step, to both Gentiles and Jews. Insight and experience were not enough. For the Gospel to take effect, Peter had to find just the right words. We should notice that it was only while he was still speaking that the Spirit fell on those listening, provoking the question and then the sacrament, bringing baptism to Gentiles (see Acts 10–11).

To tell what one sees, the preacher must tend to what, in the third book of *On Rhetoric*, Aristotle called *taxis*, *lexis*, and *hypokrisis*, to the arrangement or order (*taxis*) of the homily but also to style (*lexis*) and delivery (*hypokrisis*).[5] The terminology, which has changed over the centuries, isn't that important. What matters is that the preacher knows what to say, thinks about how to say it, and then takes care to say it well—just as Peter did, step by step.

## Pen, Paper, and Preaching: Notes and Time

But first we must treat briefly a few questions that, in all honesty, garner too much attention of both preachers and their listeners. And that is whether a homily should be written as a text and preached from a text and also how long a homily should be. Both are matters that, when a homily is excellent, matter little.

It doesn't matter, for instance, whether a homily is written out in full or only in outline, or whether the homilist preaches from the ambo or outside it. No universal principle exists; rather, it's a matter of circumstance, the preacher's comfort, and skill. Writing, however, is essential, either in the process of a homily's creation or in its delivery.

A homily preached without a text—say, for example, at an early Christmas Eve Mass with a lot of visitors and young families—can exude a liveliness, naturalness, and warmth that might be appropriate to the occasion, which preaching from a manuscript couldn't as easily accomplish. However, preaching from a written text allows for more exact expression of thought, often with more depth. When the subject of the homily is nuanced or controversial, written words help bide against unhelpful emotions or slips of phrase.

Written homilies, however, should be explicitly oral texts. That is, they should be texts meant for oral performance and not reading.[6] They may be read later, of course, but the preacher mustn't think about that when writing a homily. The text should read like the spoken voice, preserving the preacher's own unique idioms and rhythms on paper.

On the other hand, good "unwritten" homilies—those given without reading from a text—are normally born of writing. At minimum, preaching without a text demands an outline, which the preacher at some point writes down, at least in bullet point, noting what to say— such as key words or the progression of the speech. As Bishop Kenneth Untener observed, writing helps translate thought into speech, which is something preachers should do for listeners "in advance, not in front of them."[7] Often, this is precisely the problem with homilies. When they're not thought out very well, not written out, the result is drivel.

For me, writing makes unwritten homilies possible. Most of my Sunday homilies are fully written, footnoted texts, which I orally perform. Some, however, *appear* extemporaneous, but are born of a full outline committed to memory, which I preach outside the ambo. I carefully pick when to preach without a text, however, because extemporaneous homilies go smoothly for me only because I spend an enormous amount of time writing. Finding the right words on one's feet isn't easy but rather a matter of practice and habit. This is why I fully write most of my homilies. When I preach too often without a text, my extemporaneous preaching suffers, but when I rely too much on written homilies, I tend too much toward the didactic. That's just how my brain seems to work.

Every homilist ought to find what personally works, alert to circumstance, comfort, and skill. The only inexorable rule is that whatever is offered should be the preacher's best and not the byproduct of laziness or fear.

The other issue that gets too much attention is the length of homilies. Contemporary Catholic overconcern and insistence about the brevity of homilies is simply misplaced and unhelpful. The reason Catholic homilies are often unbearable has nothing to do with length but instead quality.

Normative wisdom is that the homily, due to its liturgical nature, should be brief (*Evangelii Gaudium*, 138). Bishops Kenneth Untener and Robert Morneau take that to mean that homilies should be seven to eight minutes long, and that a homily of fifteen or twenty minutes "simply rattles on and on."[8] Untener even says that a three-minute homily is "okay too."[9] Repeatedly in Catholic circles, ideal lengths of homilies are decreed—anything from three minutes to twelve minutes. But with all due respect, to insist on an ideal length measured in exact minutes is bad advice. In Catholic homiletics we seem to suffer from a timing fetish, not realizing that the duration of the homily isn't really the problem.

Yes, a Catholic homily, given its place in the liturgy, should be brief, but to say a homily must be only seven or eight minutes long is an abstract rule and frankly unhelpful. Catholic preachers need to focus more on quality than length. Listening even to short homilies can be brutal. Putting a bad preacher on the clock only adds anxiety and accentuates inability. Preachers must feel free to say what they feel called by God to say, economically and creatively. If that take five minutes, wonderful. If it takes twenty minutes, that's fine too. The only criterion is that whatever the length, the homily ought to be worth listeners' time.

Not surprisingly, it's Aristotle who's most sensible here. What matters is moderation, he said, "saying just as much as will make the thing clear."[10] When preaching once, Augustine lost track of time. "From the smell of sweat," he said, "I guess I have given quite a long talk. But because of your enthusiasm, it has not been long enough."[11] Like Aristotle, his advice was that the length of a homily depends on the situation rather than on some rule.[12]

Fr. Michael White, one of the authors of *Rebuilt*, admitted that his homilies are "about twenty minutes long." "And I do not apologize for that," he said. "The hard truth is, your church won't matter in your community until your message does."[13] This is something, frankly, we Catholics could learn from our Protestant brothers and sisters. The homily is an evangelical opportunity. Even though the Eucharist is the raison d'être of the Mass, still for many people it's the homily that forms much of their conscious experience of the Mass, especially for seekers.

Quality should be the aim, not length. As Catholic preachers, we should stop telling ourselves to "keep it short" simply because of the latest article about reduced modern attention spans or in misguided deference to the Liturgy of the Eucharist. And that's because word and sacrament belong together. The *Catechism*, quoting Vatican II's *Constitution on the Sacred Liturgy*, recognizes that the Liturgy of the Word and the Liturgy of the Eucharist are intimately connected, and in fact together form "one single act of worship" (*CCC*, 1346). As Fr. James Mallon rightly argues, we shouldn't "give in to pressure from distracted and bored parishioners to preach shorter and shorter homilies," but instead work "to create spaces for people to come to know Jesus as the living Lord."[14] The kerygma, and that alone, should be our driving principle, not some abstract ideal length. The average sitcom episode on television is a little over twenty minutes. TED Talks are "eighteen minutes or less," though the most popular talks run anywhere between ten and twenty-two minutes long.[15] This illustrates the point that it's not that people are unable listen for a certain length of time—it's that they won't listen to rubbish very long. And it's why we should just stick to Aristotle's advice and preach as long as we need to preach, just better.

# On Form: Finding Ourselves in the Story

Now back to form. When thinking about the form a homily should take, we should remember what's often said of the Church, that she is *circumdata varietate*, surrounded by variety. Augustine said preachers should be willing to "try everything" to rouse their listeners, no one form being beyond consideration.[16] This remains true today.

There are, of course, many popular homily forms, which every student of contemporary homiletics should know, each with its strengths and weaknesses. Eugene Lowry's "homiletic plot," Paul Wilson's "four pages," or David Buttrick's "moves," for example, each help a preacher think about what Aristotle called *taxis*—that is, the arrangement of what the preacher wants to say and how to say it best.[17] What really matters, however, isn't the choice of form, but that the choice of form is, as Thomas Long says, "an act of pastoral care."[18] Paying attention to sacred texts, to liturgy and liturgical time, to oneself, and especially to the world and its people, a preacher should make sure that a homily's form corresponds to the preacher's own invention, thought, focus, and function. And given the nearly endless variety of conditions of both texts and time and circumstances, the choice of form "must be custom tailored to match the particular preaching occasion."[19]

Form follows function, but here we must say more about what exactly is function, and especially from a Catholic perspective. Thomas Long says the "focus" of a sermon is what it's "about," "the central, controlling, and unifying theme." The "function" of a sermon, however, is different; it's "what the preacher hopes the sermon will create or cause to happen for the hearers."[20]

Now from a Catholic perspective, the function of a homily is not just moral or spiritual or didactic; it's also always liturgical. That is, the homily should prepare listeners for an encounter with Christ in the Eucharist, inspiring prayer similar to the one offered by the two disciples on the road to Emmaus in Luke's gospel. "Stay with us," they begged the mysteriously hidden Christ after he'd preached to them along the way, before they recognized him in the breaking of the bread (Lk 24:29). That's the Catholic difference, what separates Catholic preaching from Protestant, that the basic function of all Catholic homilies is to attract listeners to Christ in the Eucharist, Sunday by Sunday, and even day by day.

So the function of a Catholic homily is always eucharistic, helping listeners encounter Jesus in the Blessed Sacrament. But how best does a preacher accomplish that? How does a homilist help listeners move seamlessly from the Liturgy of the Word to the Liturgy of the Eucharist, experiencing them as two parts of an organic whole, one naturally leading to the other? Here's where it pays to know about inductive preaching and the power of narrative. Because, quite simply, it's how best to carry listeners from one part of the Mass to the other.

Inductive preaching in our day is often associated with Fred Craddock, particularly with his book *As One without Authority*. There he makes a key distinction between deductive and inductive preaching, emphatically urging the latter.

Deductive preaching proceeds by "stating the thesis, breaking it down into points of subtheses, explaining and illustrating these points, and applying them to the particular situations of the hearers."[21] An example of deduction in Catholic preaching would be if a homily began something such as, "The readings today teach us about the Blessed Sacrament of the Eucharist, which is the Body and Blood of Christ, with his soul and divinity." Stating the thesis just so, the preacher would go on to support it by referring to both scripture and theological tradition, perhaps adding an illustration before concluding with an appeal to devotion, repentance, or even conversion.

Inductive preaching, however, works in the opposite direction, "from the particulars of experience that have a familiar ring in the listener's ear to a general truth or conclusion."[22] An inductive homily might, therefore, begin this way:

> My niece was born just a few days ago, and all she does, it seems, is eat.
>
> She and her mother are inseparable, that tiny baby tucked safely in her arms. Born, she wants to eat. Born, she's drawn to her mother, because she knows that with her mother is found the food she needs. Just like us, born in the font of baptism and drawn to this altar, to this mother, the Church. Because we're hungry.
>
> My niece, all she wants to do, it seems, is eat, safe in her mother's arms.

Now what's the difference between these two ways of preaching? Deduction gets to the point right away, stating the truth clearly, which the preacher means to deliver. It presents the information directly and candidly. It's no-nonsense and didactic. Induction, however, begins with a relatable experience or with some personal understanding that listeners can easily recognize (such as newborn babies and hunger) and then relates that experience to an experience of the faith (the experience of Baptism and desire for the Eucharist). Both forms, of course, can facilitate truth. It's just that one begins with dogma, the other with experience.

So why is inductive preaching better? Because, unlike deductive preaching, which presents material directly as information or data to be either accepted or rejected, inductive preaching allows listeners to discover themselves *within* the subject of the homily itself.

Per our example, listeners understand immediately that newborn babies eat a lot. And even without being able to locate it in the gospels or in Paul, most will have some faint associative notion of Baptism as a sort of birth, something often celebrated at infancy, and they will also faintly know (even if they don't know why) that one receives the Eucharist only after Baptism. Either faint or clear, this loosely associated knowledge helps listeners begin to see these two sacraments in terms of birth and hunger, seeing Baptism and Eucharist as the supernatural extension of a natural phenomenon. And from that, listeners may begin to reflect on their own hunger, not just physical but spiritual. They may then begin to think about why they're sitting in the pew—that maybe they're hungry too. And all this will occur just moments before they see the Body and Blood of Christ and hear the words of invitation: "Blessed are those called to the supper of the Lamb."[23]

If the focus of the homily is the Eucharist, and if its function is to help listeners encounter Christ in the Eucharist, then helping listeners recognize their hunger for the Eucharist, by talking in a relatable way about natural hunger, is better use of homiletic time than simply stating a theological thesis and supporting it with proofs. Craddock said that inductive preaching was the better way to preach today, because the "inductive process is fundamental to the American way of life."[24] Less responsive, he said, to direct appeals to authority, we're more conditioned to the presentation of experiences to which we can relate.

From a Catholic perspective, however, there's an even deeper reason that inductive preaching works best. Preaching, as Craddock said, from particular truths to general truth helps listeners find themselves within the experience of the liturgy itself, in the mystery itself. Such preaching doesn't just teach listeners the truth of the Eucharist. It helps them hunger for it by seeing the hunger they already feel in light of the food of the Eucharist. It helps prepare listeners to lift up their hearts.

Now inductive preaching is accomplished by means of narrative—that is, by stories or by preaching that is "narrativelike."[25] When Aristotle talked about induction, he talked about what he called "paradigms," of which, he said, were two kinds: comparison (*parabolē*) and fables (*logoi*).[26] Our sample homily, which began by reflecting on a newborn baby, is an example of comparison—the newborn's physical hunger is compared with our own spiritual hunger. Fables, of course, are more explicitly stories, and they can be either personal or biblical or historical. But they are not mere illustrations or anecdotes. Rather, a narrative or story is the subject itself, not just its proof.

But what does that look like? Take, for instance, the Fourth Sunday in Ordinary Time, Year B. And assume that the homilist wants to preach on the first reading and the gospel, Deuteronomy 18:15–20 and Mark 1:21–28. The Old Testament reading foretells a prophet like Moses, meant to succeed the great Hebrew leader and to whom the People of God must listen. And the gospel records the first public healing miracle Jesus performed at the synagogue in Capernaum, at which the people were amazed by his authority. Now how might one preach these texts inductively by means of narrative?

Maybe the preacher begins in another part of the Bible altogether, such as Acts 3. He could begin by retelling the story of how Peter and John healed the disabled man begging outside the Beautiful Gate. Like any good storyteller, the preacher could accentuate details, such as how the beggar "leaped up" and walked into the temple with Peter and John, "jumping and praising God" (Acts 3:8), probably for the first time in his life, and perhaps with tears in his eyes. Describing the crowd's reaction, how they gathered around Peter, perhaps at exactly that dramatic moment, the preacher could say, "Peter knew he needed to explain himself." That sets the scene, allowing the preacher to introduce Peter's defense: "For Moses said: 'A prophet like me will the LORD, your God, raise up for you from among your own kindred; that is the one to whom you shall listen'"—which, of course, is Deuteronomy 18:15.

But why begin the homily this way? Because it puts the first reading in a narrative context. By starting with the story from Acts, the passage from Deuteronomy goes from being a distinct reading to part of a larger story. It becomes part of a narrative that most listeners will want to follow toward some sort of resolution. Now the preacher can talk about the specific context of Deuteronomy 18:15–20, but cast in terms of prophecy and hope. Talking about how this passage has been read in terms of figures such as Joshua and Samuel and the enduring hope of Israel, the homilist can soon make his way to John the Baptist and to the question put to him: "Are you the Prophet?" (Jn 1:21). From there, all the preacher needs to do is take the Baptist's own answer to that question and then look to Jesus, who dared to say that it was he whom Moses wrote about (see Jn 5:46). This prepares listeners to think more profoundly about the authority people saw in Jesus in that synagogue in Capernaum and about why they were so intrigued, not only by the miracle but also by the power of his words, because they were obeyed even by demons.

But then, paying attention to liturgical time, the preacher might ask aloud why the Church offers this gospel reading on this particular Sunday early in Ordinary Time. After celebrating Advent and Christmas, when we prepared for and celebrated the coming of Christ; after celebrating the Epiphany, when we remembered that Christ is for all people; and after celebrating the baptism of Christ, when we recalled the Father's command to listen to his Son; and then after two Sundays of stories about the call of the disciples, perhaps the preacher needs simply to ask listeners, "Why do you think, after all this, the Church wants to tell us this story about the words and deeds of Jesus?" And here, if the homilist needs to help people find the right answer, he can simply quote the psalm refrain appointed for the day: "If today you hear his voice, harden not your hearts" (see Ps 95:8). When the texts are placed in a narrative relationship and within liturgical time, suddenly the gospel reading comes alive as an evangelical invitation to respond to Jesus, present and active today.

Now what is accomplished by preaching these readings this way? By dramatically putting the readings in a narrative context, making use of other biblical texts as needed, the readings are made more like a story with a beginning, middle, and end, which listeners naturally like. But more than that, paying attention to liturgical time invites listeners to imagine how they fit within that same narrative. The prophecy from Deuteronomy, fulfilled in the Christ celebrated liturgically, becomes suddenly relevant, and so too the command that we harden not our hearts, all just a few weeks before Lent.

The value of inductive preaching isn't that it's more relatable and less boring. It's that it has a unique way of putting listeners inside the narrative itself. That's why it's particularly valuable in Catholic preaching. Because from the Catholic perspective, the narrative of scripture hasn't ended but instead extends into the life of the Church, historically and sacramentally. Inductive preaching helps listeners appropriate the stories of scripture, not as detached reports of some dislocated past but as earlier scenes in a story still being told—a story that includes them. Inductive preaching enlivens the past of scripture and reveals the depth and purpose of present liturgies. Ultimately, it makes hope and grace described in the liturgy more real, inviting listeners to sing with angels and archangels and all the hosts and powers of heaven.

# The Joy of Speaking

Following form, the preacher must next consider style and delivery, what Aristotle called *lexis* and *hypokrisis*. Concern for style in the rhetorical tradition was always important. Cicero, for instance, said it was style that made the orator.[27] For Aristotle, style was primarily a matter of clarity—that is, the proper choice of words, metaphors, and similes. It was about avoiding unnecessarily clunky, complex words, being grammatically correct and concise, as well as paying attention to the rhythm of sentences and so on.[28] All of it, for Aristotle, was as essential as the argument itself.

Delivery, however, got shorter shrift in Aristotle's writings. He thought it a vulgar necessity, something a speaker needed to think about only because of the irrational "corruption of the audience." Only because listeners couldn't easily follow the argument, Aristotle thought, did the speaker have to perform a certain way in order to sway the emotions of the crowd. Here Aristotle's philosophical snobbery is on full display. Still, he was right. Style can be learned and practiced, but delivery, less so. Delivery is basically acting, he thought, and therefore as much the product of natural talent as anything else.[29]

So saying anything meaningful about delivery is harder. Phillips Brooks wrote, "I believe in the true elocution teacher, as I believe in the existence of Halley's Comet, which comes into sight of this earth once in about seventy-six years."[30] Preachers should beware of promises made by innumerable books and courses on public speaking. For instance, on page 1 of *Stand and Deliver*, a book put out by Dale Carnegie Training, the reader is promised: "You can transform yourself into an effective public speaker almost instantly."[31] This, of course, is nonsense, a sales pitch.

Speaking well just isn't that easy. There are principles that can be coached, a little, and it is something that should be studied. Remember, though, that Socrates said it was like cooking, something that required knack.[32] Or as Aristotle insisted, it's an art learned by habituation. And so that means the best way to learn how to preach is to get in the kitchen and start cooking, to use Socrates's image, preferably alongside a master chef. It's best to get into the studio and just start painting, thinking less about creating a masterpiece or what critics will say, and more about the art itself and truth of expression. Learning by doing is how to learn preaching and delivery. Books alone won't help, not without repeated trial and error and the support of your fellow preachers.

However, before getting into the pulpit or racing to the ambo, a little preliminary advice is appropriate. Writing an exhaustive manual on good *lexis* and *hypokrisis* in preaching isn't what this chapter or this book is about. Nonetheless, there are some more immediately relevant pieces of advice worthy of both preaching novices and veterans alike, things preachers could think about and work on right away, and which would have an immediate impact on the quality of Catholic preaching.

The first bit of advice is about what Bishop Untener called the "pulpit tone." He said it's one of the "demons" of preaching. It's when the pitch and inflection in a preacher's voice are radically different in the pulpit than when speaking elsewhere. And it's more than a "minor matter," he said, because the "pulpit tone is perceived by the listeners as artificial and can get in the way of a good homily."[33]

Countless preachers would instantly go from boring to better if they noticed and then eliminated "pulpit tone." Minding the intimacy of the preaching event and the humanity of the medium—Pope Francis likened it to a mother's conversation, remember—the preacher should feel free to speak with the immediacy of genuine personality and without the distance of artificially formal intonation (*Evangelii Gaudium*, 139). No matter the importance of speaking clearly and loudly, the preacher's voice mustn't be artificial. Like all good art, preaching should appear natural. The preacher's personality must clearly show.

Another good piece of advice is about what Aristotle called "appropriateness" or "propriety." Style, he said, "is appropriate if it expresses emotion and character and is proportional to the subject matter."[34] For the preacher, this means respecting the overall *pathos* and effect of the various moods in play during the preaching event.

What's the mood of scripture, for instance? Are we reading Psalm 88 or Psalm 150? What's the mood of the liturgy? Are we preaching at a funeral or at the kids' First Communion? What's the mood of the people? Did the local team win the Super Bowl, or was there recently a school shooting? Bubbly jokes don't really work on Good Friday, nor do diatribes at Easter. A good preacher will be able to read all this instantly, making changes to everything from content to tone of voice. When the preacher's words and manner are appropriate, he will be heard and not rejected as clueless or insensitive.

This doesn't mean, however, that the preacher is entirely passive to the moods and emotions of the moment. Sometimes the preacher's task is to nudge listeners into emotions more appropriate to what the Church is trying to teach or commemorate. Sometimes the preacher's job is to put people in the mood.

John Henry Newman's harrowing sermon, for example, titled "The Crucifixion," begins with long, detailed descriptions of animal cruelty, child abuse, and abuse of the innocent and elderly. He begins by deliberately stirring up listeners' most visceral emotions. But he does so only to pause near the end of his startling opening to say, "But what is all this to the suffering of the holy Jesus, which we bear to read of as a matter of course!"[35]

Now what was Newman doing? Rather forcefully, he was moving a likely complacent congregation nearer the *pathos* of the biblical and liturgical moment of the Crucifixion. Now I wouldn't recommend Newman's strategy of mentioning things such as child abuse today, of course, because the preacher doesn't know what sort of trauma doing so may inadvertently revisit upon some listeners. We are these days blessedly more sensitive. Nonetheless, the principle remains that the preacher should be able not only to respond to the *pathos* of the preaching moment but also influence it.

The preacher should also pay close attention to the rhythm of words, discovering what's pleasing to the ear. Words and phrases and sentences, long and short, should be put together in ways that bear some sort of followable pattern. Prose rhythm is less metrical than poetry, but they both exhibit patterns the ear wants to follow. Behind this, at least for me, is somewhat complicated mathematics, but fortunately it's not important that the preacher understand it. If we are speaking our native languages, this should come naturally. It does help, though, to read good prose and poetry and listen to good music. Normally, that's training enough to learn about rhythm in speech patterns.

A homilist should also develop a personal system of writing, almost like code, to help remember and execute the appropriate rhythm of speech. Homilists using texts will sometimes use ellipses or spacing; sometimes they'll write certain words in bold or italics. My homily texts, for instance, are riddled with hyphens. Speaking without a text, the preacher mentally will mark out pauses and turning points in advance, using words or images as mental signposts.

Methods are idiosyncratic; no one method is intrinsically better than another. What matters is that a preacher has thought about it, worked at it, and practiced it, and that when the time comes, knows the routine, every step by heart. That's how a homilist's words become like notes of music and preaching like a song.

This is what I think Augustine meant by *hilaritas*, being able to offer people words of faith "with joy," which he said was a defining characteristic of good preaching.[36] It's what Phillips Brooks said about elocution, that "your oratory must be your own intelligent delight in what you are doing."[37] Being joyful is the origin of style and delivery. Being oneself and not too stuffy and overly formal, minding the moods and emotions of the moment, paying attention to the music of language: when all that is put together and practiced, preaching becomes less something forced and conscious and more something simply experienced, like music. Preaching is about getting others to dance to the music of the Gospel, because you're able to show them how much fun it is.

# A Noble Thing

But what finally is the point? Why bother with form, style, and delivery? What good does it do listeners? Why is a well-crafted and well-delivered narrative so powerful? What's the bigger picture?

To answer this, let me share with you a children's story. In *The House at Pooh Corner*, there is a famous story about Winnie-the-Pooh and Piglet. The morning after Owl's house collapsed in a storm, Pooh Bear shared with Piglet a new song he'd made up. Like the author, A. A. Milne, Pooh was quite a poet, always making up rhymes and songs. This song was about Piglet's courage, which he had shown the day before when, being a very small animal, he escaped Owl's ruined house through the letter box in the door. "O gallant Piglet (PIGLET)! Ho!" Pooh Bear sang, seven verses in all.[38] Hearing it, Piglet didn't quite know what to think. He "said nothing," the story goes, "but just stood and glowed." He couldn't believe he'd been as brave as that:

> "Did I really do all that?" he said at last.
>
> "Well," said Pooh, "in poetry—in a piece of poetry— well, you *did* it, Piglet, because the poetry says you did. And that's how people know."

Slowly Pooh's song began to change Piglet. "Piglet sighed with happiness," the story says, "and began to think about himself. He was BRAVE."[39]

But his bravery was soon tested. Eeyore, who had been faithfully searching the Hundred Acre Wood for another house for Owl, finally found one, only it wasn't entirely new. Unbeknownst to Eeyore, it was Piglet's house. As everyone began to realize the mistake, but not wanting to disappoint Eeyore, they awkwardly looked to Piglet, wondering what he would say. Surely Piglet would put a stop to it. Surely he'd protest, "That's my house!" and correct the mistake. But that's not what he did. Rather, Piglet did something else entirely:

> And then Piglet did a Noble Thing, and he did it in a sort of dream, while he was thinking of all the wonderful words Pooh had hummed about him.
>
> "Yes, it's just the house for Owl," he said grandly. "And I hope he'll be very happy in it." And then he gulped twice, because he had been very happy in it himself.[40]

Piglet remembered Pooh's wonderful words in a sort of dream because they had got stuck in his heart. Because the song had made him "glow," Piglet did a "Noble Thing." Pooh's song changed Piglet. The story moved him. Inspired by the story, Piglet acted in charity and sacrifice, like a Christian.

That's the bigger picture. Winnie-the-Pooh teaches us that beyond focus, function, and form, beyond style and delivery, the fruit of preaching is the noble thing, the gracious and charitable act, often sacrificial, which words can inspire. Paul wrote, "Let the word of Christ dwell in you richly, as in all wisdom you teach and admonish one another, singing psalms, hymns, and spiritual songs with gratitude in your hearts to God" (Col 3:16). Here the apostle and the bear teach the same truth. The Gospel has power to enter listeners' minds and hearts and change them for the better. As Pooh said, "Poetry and Hums aren't things you get, they're things which get *you*."[41] That's why we should take care how we preach the Gospel, because of the power of narrative to inspire Christlike acts of love.

When Peter preached his first sermon at Pentecost, those who listened "were cut to the heart" and asked, "What are we to do?" (Acts 2:37). The sign of fruitful preaching is that it readies listeners to act in a more moral and spiritual way—that it inspires them, as Pope Francis said, to go forth together as "missionary disciples," becoming people "who bear fruit and rejoice" (*Evangelii Gaudium*, 24).

But that demands we become better preachers. It demands we work a little harder, like Pooh Bear, on our poems and hums and songs.

# 7.

# THE WAY
# OF CRITICISM

The way of fools seems right in their own eyes, but those
who listen to advice are the wise.

—Proverbs 12:15

Preaching can either inspire or aggravate, so we had best be ready for
both. "One must not forget," Fred Craddock wrote, "that there are two
kinds of preaching difficult to hear: poor preaching and good preaching."[1] Both provoke response. As Cicero and Augustine taught, the task
of the orator is to teach, to delight, and finally to sway. For the preacher,
that means inspiring obedience to the Gospel.[2] But that's not easy.

That's because ever since Adam and Eve, we've been resisters of
truth. Like our forebears wandering in the desert epochs ago, we remain
a murmuring people. Grumbling, complaining, prevaricating, flattering,
outright rebelling: we are a stubborn species, a people of proud, hardened hearts. It's why Augustine said listeners often seek out even the
tiniest faults and smallest of vices in the words and character of their
preachers, because it gives them an excuse.[3]

To criticize the preacher is a primeval phenomenon. It will always be
part of one's ministry. If Moses and Jesus and countless others weren't
spared it, there is no reason we should expect otherwise. If a preacher doesn't occasionally receive criticism, it's likely because no one is

listening, or because they've given up caring one way or the other about anything the preacher says. This, of course, worse than criticism, is the death of preaching.

Now there are two types of criticism. One type of criticism is basically constructive, born of love for both God and the preacher. The other type is adversarial, born of that deeper resistance, hardhearted and devilish. We should be grateful for both types of criticism, however, and open to each, but in different ways. Too much at once can be harmful, but in proportion, criticism can be helpful. "A parish of critics would be killing," Phillips Brooks wrote, "but a critic here and there is a tonic."[4] Constructive criticism is valuable because it keeps us honest, helping improve the art of preaching. Adversarial criticism is valuable because it conforms the preacher to the Cross, making one's homily more like a eucharistic preface: words before the sacrifice.

Constructive criticism is helpful because it makes us better preachers. When accomplished athletes study film after a game, they're not looking for highlights but instead for mistakes. A player who never listened to coaches, never took criticism, probably wouldn't learn much, or play much either. For athletes, receiving criticism is part of learning the game. The same is true for preaching. As good athletes want to know their mistakes, so should preachers want to know their foibles. Such criticism is valuable, which is why it's called "constructive." It's criticism that builds up instead of tears down.

For the preacher, though, there is something deeper at stake. And that's spiritual blindness. Criticism and praise are hard to process together. If the preacher resists all praise, it quickly leads to despair, thinking oneself the world's worst preacher. On the other hand, if the preacher resists all criticism, all that remains is the desire for praise. For the preacher, this is deadly, since human praise is so blinding.

John's gospel is clear. Jesus said desire for human praise was the reason some people didn't recognize him. Early in his ministry, responding to those arguing with him about a man he healed on the Sabbath, Jesus asked them, "How can you believe, when you accept praise from one another and do not seek the praise that comes from the only God?" (Jn 5:44). In John, the fundamental explanation for why some people believed Jesus and others didn't was that those who failed to believe "preferred human praise to the glory of God" (Jn 12:43). That's why eyes were blinded and hearts hardened: because human praise was desired above all else.

Hence the warning over the centuries from preachers of all kinds about what Augustine called the earthly city's love of self.[5] It's found everywhere, and if we're honest, sometimes it's in abundance among us preachers. So if we're spiritually serious about preaching, we should accept criticism that comes our way, because it keeps us from going spiritually blind.

"I am nearly always dissatisfied with the address that I give," Augustine once admitted. His words, he said, never quite did his thoughts justice.[6] Comfortable with criticism and self-aware: that's the mark of a good preacher. It's important to acknowledge openly weakness, little faults, tics, failures, misunderstandings, and even sin. We preachers, as the old saying goes, shouldn't want to hover aloof "ten feet above contradiction," but instead we should want to know the truth about ourselves.[7] And although it shouldn't have to be said, it must: this is true for everyone, from popes to prelates to pastors to parochial vicars to deacons. "Bishops, too, have to learn," Cyprian said.[8] If ordination doesn't magically confer preaching skills upon deacons and priests, the same goes for bishops. All of us would do well to embrace criticism a little better. Because that's how we'll preach Christ more clearly and more boldly.

We shouldn't fear that if we open the door to criticism, somehow our credibility and preaching will suffer. Quite the contrary. It was John the Baptist, remember, who said, "He must increase; I must decrease" (Jn 3:30). His preaching didn't suffer with that attitude. He embraced humility because he knew his purpose, which is the same as ours—to point to the Lamb of God and then get out of the way.

# Take It Personally

We should take criticism well so that it helps and doesn't just hurt.

Bishop Kenneth Untener was right that the preacher shouldn't put too much store in anything said immediately after Mass.[9] What's said in the narthex is usually compromised by all sorts of things such as politeness, clerical deference, and the hundred other people waiting to be greeted. It's not a time when one can receive criticism in a way that's helpful. In this situation, the preacher should invite the person to make an appointment or write an email and promise to talk about things in more depth another time. This is, of course, something of a deflection, but it helps separate much of the wheat from the chaff. And in the bustle of a Sunday, it's often necessary.

Also, generally speaking, immediate reactions typically aren't very good. Whenever you've gotten upset, for instance, how often was the first thing you said also the best thing you said? Probably not very often. It's just the way we are as emotional, rational beings. Most of the time, we must calm down, count to ten, take a breath or two before we can even begin to think straight, much less speak well.

Nor should we worry too much about what people may or may not be thinking during the homily itself. Augustine talked about this: perceiving apathy during the homily, preachers can sometimes "begin to falter and feel ground down because all our efforts seem for nothing."[10] Preaching in the fifth century was a far more raucous affair than it is today, listeners often voicing pleasure or displeasure immediately. Shouting, clapping, weeping, jeering: ancient preachers usually didn't have to wait long for feedback.[11] Today listeners are more sedate, of course, but still the preacher can sense a congregation's moods. Both frenetic excitement and tomblike silence can affect the homilist. It's something a skilled speaker ought to know how to handle in the moment, knowing how to stay on course. Never doubt either your homily or your vocation before you've even finished speaking. Cut yourself a little more slack than that.

As Untener wisely said, the most valuable feedback, good or bad, "comes days, weeks, months later."[12] That's what preachers should take far more seriously, even prize: criticism that's aged, not what's given either in the moment or in the immediate aftermath of a homily. Almost always, when someone reaches out to a preacher about a homily that has long gone from the minds of most listeners, what's offered is the gift of genuine reflection. And that's wisdom that helps.

Trusted voices give valuable criticism, and parishioners' voices should be trusted. If a preacher is unable to receive criticism from parishioners or other invested lay listeners, then there are bigger problems than just preaching. No one is above charitable reproach. Nathan called David to task; Paul got in Peter's face (see 2 Sm 12:7; Gal 2:11). If they weren't spared the medicine of criticism, no one is. Grabbing coffee with a parishioner, taking a letter or email to prayer, following up if necessary, listening to the People of God: these are pastoral practices we homilists must accept, if we understand preaching to be a sacred privilege and not a right.

Criticism is best when it occurs naturally and personally. Surveys or regularly scheduled meetings, although not entirely without value, don't offer the same depth of reflection nor the passion that comes from a parishioner who *needs* to speak with you. Formalized feedback is data. Talking to a person is sacramental. If scripture offers any clue, the Holy Spirit prefers the latter. Jesus said he abides within his people, and especially in the least of his brothers and sisters or when just two or three gather together (see Mt 25:40; 18:20). If this is true, then a preacher ought not hide from listeners, even when they criticize. Because they are Christ and have a word to preach too.

We must recover the biblical practice of fraternal correction (see Jas 5:19–20). Because of the grace and presence of Christ promised to dwell among believers in the Spirit, accepting criticism willingly is an act of faith. More sacramental than any survey or some regularly scheduled meeting, taking criticism as it comes naturally, nudged by the Spirit, fosters better homiletics. It helps preaching bear more deeply the fruit of dialogue and less the processed reflections of marketing and focus groups.

That doesn't mean getting feedback and criticism should be unintentional, but simply more organic and less produced. That small congregation of parishioners with whom you pray the Liturgy of the Hours, for instance, will talk about the homily and ask you pointed questions, but within the afterglow charity of prayer. The subtle but significant difference is that it's not a meeting to "talk to Father about the homily" but rather a conversation. And almost always these ad hoc conversations will be from the heart, and always more memorable and valuable.

Clergy should be intentional about scheduling meetings to talk about homilies. One of the biggest obstacles to the renewal of Catholic preaching is the conspiracy of silence surrounding the homily, in rectories and parish offices all throughout the Church. We may on occasion talk about the poor state of preaching in safely vague abstraction, or we may even talk about some notoriously bad or particularly gifted colleague over dinner. Yet rarely do clergy come together intentionally to talk about preaching, offering one another constructive criticism and mutual support. We act as if seminary and ordination gave us all the tools and training we'll ever need to be effective preachers. We're afraid to practice fraternal correction, either to give it or receive it. That's why bad preaching has become a cultural feature of the Catholic Church and why it feels as if nothing will change.

But it can change. If we really want to transform the culture of bad preaching in the Catholic Church into a renaissance of good preaching, every homilist should seek out communities of charitable criticism, among parishioners and especially fellow clergy. Something like Untener's Saginaw Program, conducted preferably at the parish or deanery level rather than at the diocesan or national level, could create conditions favorable to genuine renewal—if done well.

The Saginaw Program, as outlined in Untener's book *Preaching Better*, is simple. A group of homilists share video recordings of one another's homilies, and transcripts are provided if there isn't a text. Then, for two hours, fellow homilists offer honest feedback about everything from content to delivery. Untener enjoyed the good fortune of having a former copy editor on his staff, which enabled him to add an expert voice into the mix. He also invited a trained theologian into the group in addition to soliciting laypeople to watch the homilies and offer feedback by mail.[13]

The benefit of something like the Saginaw Program is that it offers constructive technical advice—that is, helpful criticism about the tools of the trade. Whereas the criticism brought by parishioners and other invested lay listeners will often be more spiritually and prophetically rich and probing, criticism brought by fellow clergy will be more about know-how and knack.

The number of times a homilist says "um," pet phrases that need to be retired, bad habits of posture or gesture, theology that ought to be clarified, how to treat difficult subjects pastorally as a team: all of it is up for discussion at meetings like this. In so many other professions there are processes of peer review; Untener talks about airline check pilots as an example.[14] Why not do the same for preaching? Why not take the art of preaching so seriously that we'll work together to make one another better? Why are we satisfied with sighing and groaning and behind-the-back complaining about all our poor preaching? Why don't we do something about it? Or do we not think it all that important?

Criticism must remain personal. We must resist the contemporary Catholic proclivity to bureaucratize things, to put somebody in a diocesan office to churn out unhelpful mail and sign people up for workshops. Formal programs designed to help homilists grow in the art of preaching serve a useful purpose, of course. However, what brings about genuine renewal are not impersonal programs and initiatives but simply changed daily habits of individual preachers. And that only happens locally when people begin to take things personally.

That's why something like the Saginaw Program would work best at the parish level under the direction of a pastor, helping his parochial vicars and deacons, and they helping him. Or perhaps it would work well at the deanery level, the bishop appointing someone to facilitate homily discussion sessions for small groups of clergy. Care should be taken, however, to keep such discussions at the grassroots level, because the higher such initiatives begin institutionally, the less personal they are and less effective.

Genuine renewal, which is both born of the Spirit and lasting, is often not a matter of scope and scale. Renewal may eventually set fire to the whole Church, but it always begins small, sometimes with just twelve people. The same will be true of preaching. Real renewal is born of spiritual dialogue *cor ad cor loquitor*, spoken from heart to heart. It's why criticism is best taken personally, because, like the act of preaching itself, it's more human and more spiritual. It's dialogue instead of data.

# Change Is Hard

But criticism is not an end in itself. A coach points out a player's mistakes not to relish in misery but so the player will make the changes necessary to improve, and so the team will have a better chance to win the game. The same is true for preaching. We embrace criticism to embrace change, so that we can better play the game of mission and evangelism.

The immediate purpose of intentionally accepting criticism is to discover those foibles and fears that hinder good preaching, everything from stage fright to sin. It's a practice that when embraced over time will go a long way to remove bad habits. But, of course, not always.

It is the case that no matter how many books, no matter how many workshops and programs on preaching are available, no matter how hard a person tries, sometimes improvement won't happen. True for teachers and pilots and athletes, it's true for preachers too. There are, and always will be, some preachers who just aren't very good, even at their best. This is why we ought to take Fred Craddock's advice to heart, as hard as it may at first sound:

> Some ministers may arrive at the painful conclusion that they cannot preach; at least, not very well. If that conclusion is supported by knowing and caring friends and peers, some form of ministry without pulpit should be sought. Such a person is no less a minister, and the church should say so clearly. As important as preaching is, neither the pulpit nor the church is served by the view that only those who preach are really ministers. That attitude has kept some too long in the pulpit and caused others whose abilities lay elsewhere to abandon the ministry altogether.[15]

Now for Catholics this is a countercultural recommendation. Yet it's not beyond the realm of possibility. The Church clearly prefers that a homilist at a liturgy also be that liturgy's principal celebrant, *ordinarily*. However, "if appropriate" or for a "just cause," preaching may be assigned to someone other than the celebrant, so long as the person is ordained.[16] This, of course, happens all over the Church every Sunday already, every time a deacon steps up to preach during Mass.

However, this allowance given by the Church doesn't exist solely for the sake of deacons and visiting clergy. When putting together the preaching schedule in the parish, too often it's treated like a chore to be distributed evenly among the workers. Too often clergy assume they have some sort of right to preach, taking offense at not being given equal opportunity along with everyone else. Sometimes clergy suffer the pangs of wounded dignity and point in protest to all their training and degrees. Preaching quickly becomes about them rather than about the reason they got all those degrees in the first place. Quickly it becomes a matter of ego instead of mission and evangelism.

If we are to take seriously the call of the New Evangelization, then we must, as John Paul II taught, look at everything from the "viewpoint of evangelization" (*Redemptoris Missio*, 33). And that means *everything*. We must rethink the way we run our parishes and dioceses, the way we catechize and initiate children and adults, the way we offer youth ministry and pastoral care, and so much more. As James Mallon put it, we should stop subjecting Christ's mission to the Church's infrastructure but instead change the Church's infrastructure to serve Christ's mission.[17] Everything we do should be questioned, every structure scrutinized and reformed, all with an eye to evangelism and to the reality that our first, most urgent mission is to make disciples. Letting go once and for all our caretaker mentality, realizing that homogenous Catholic cultures no longer exist—that even many cradle Catholics wallow unformed in old, dying folkways and not in the vibrancy of Gospel life—we Catholic ministers, ordained and lay, must wake up. We must be willing to jettison the many old, tired ways in which the institutional Catholic Church still lumbers along.

And that means rethinking the way we approach preaching, quitting the anti-evangelical notion that somehow every member of the clergy has equal right to preach simply by virtue of ordination and faculties. To think that every ordained member of the clergy has equal right to preach is to think that ministry is about status rather than mission. And that's simply wrong.

If the homily, as Pope Paul VI taught, is truly an "instrument of evangelization," then the way we go about preaching must change

(*Evangelii Nuntiandi*, 43).Thinking about the homily evangelically, pastors should be willing also to think strategically about homilies preached in the parish. This means that preaching ought to be conditioned and ordered to mission and evangelism, which is not simply a matter of content, form, and delivery but also a matter of personnel. A coach doesn't rotate players at random; rather, he or she puts the right players in the game at the right time. Because it's the coach's job to give the team the best chance of victory by making the strategic decisions necessary to win.

Pastors should be like coaches. Part of their job as shepherds is to think strategically about how best to make and grow disciples in the communities entrusted to them by God and the bishops. Pastors must sometimes make difficult strategic decisions about who should and shouldn't preach, decisions they should feel empowered, even obliged, to make, because it does little good for either the preacher or the kingdom of God to continue to take the warm-body approach to preaching. We must think better and differently, more with an eye to the kingdom than to ourselves.

We must embrace hard change. Pope Francis challenged each of us to become missionary disciples, to bring "the word of Jesus to the inmost soul of our cities" (*Evangelii Gaudium*, 74). But that's easier said than done. If we are to be true heralds of Christ, decreasing so that God might increase, genuinely open not only to heartfelt praise but also to charitable criticism, then we ought also to embrace difficult and even humbling change for the sake of mission. Like Paul, we should be able to swallow pride and simply rejoice that Christ is being proclaimed, no matter who is preaching (see Phil 1:18).

# Deeper Resistance

As I said, not all criticism is constructive, nor all of it charitable. A coach is one thing, a heckler, quite another. Some criticism is born of love, some of misunderstanding, some of ignorance. Some criticism, though, is born of rebellion, of that original willfulness that has always belonged to this wayward world. That is, sometimes opposition is just that: opposition. Born of a deeper resistance, some criticism is purely adversarial. Here the preacher must call on deeper resources, because this criticism isn't constructive but satanic.

The homilist should bear in mind that preaching and martyrdom are two modes of the one kerygma of the kingdom of God. When Stephen finished preaching, for instance, his listeners were "infuriated, and they ground their teeth at him" (Acts 7:54). Killing him, however, did not silence him but instead perfected his witness. His testimony remained. That's the strange thing about martyrdom, that although in outward form it appears to be defeat, it's really victory. When the Word of God is spoken in the world, it is sometimes challenged and scourged and crucified. But it always rises.

Words are more powerful when joined to sacrifice, because sacrifice shows there is love and truth more determinative and stronger than power, politics, or tribes. Christian witness has always been more than mere words, because God's wisdom is Christ, that stumbling block wisdom of the Cross, which is love and mercy given in death even for the wicked (see 1 Cor 1:18–21). At the heart of the Christian faith is sacrifice, which is action and not merely speech. That's why it doesn't only matter what you say as a Christian but also what you do, and more importantly, what God does through you.

At the beginning of the *Martyr Act of Lyons and Vienne* is the story of a young man named Vettius Epagathus. As the persecution began, so the story goes, young Vettius, filled with indignation, "requested a hearing to speak in defense of the Christians." As soon as he got to court, however, he was immediately shouted down. Everything he wanted to say, he soon discovered didn't matter. The Roman prefect didn't care about Vettius's finely worded defense. Rather, he wanted to know only one thing:

> The prefect dismissed the just request that he had put forward and merely asked him if he too were a Christian. When he admitted he was in the clearest tones, he too was accepted into the ranks of the martyrs. Called the Christians' advocate, he possessed the Advocate within him . . . which he demonstrated by the fullness of his love, consenting as he did to lay

down his life in defence of his fellow Christians. He was and
is a true disciple of Christ, *following the Lamb wherever he goes*.[18]

In the end, Vettius's words didn't matter. Ultimately the martyr's con-
fession of Christ (*homologia*) is more valuable than mere apologetics
(*apologoumenos*), sacrifice more than sermons. Our words mean little if
we're not also willing to suffer for them.[19] It's the final measure of all
Christian speech.

This brings us back to how we think about preaching and to the
adversarial criticism born of that deeper rebellion. There remains in
each heart some element of hostility toward God, even in the hearts of
the faithful. Fred Craddock put it mildly when he said, "Most people
want grace but not so amazing."[20] Paul, however, was far more blunt and
realistic, asking the Galatians, "Have I become your enemy by telling
you the truth?" (Gal 4:16). Eventually, it's an experience that comes to
every faithful preacher, standing alone against the stubborn hardness
of sin. Sometimes counted a "deceiver" even though "truthful," the
preacher is tasked with holding the "unfeigned love" of God within
the storms of hatred and opposition, "rejoicing" even when "chastised"
(2 Cor 6:1–10).

Preaching the Gospel of Christ, we should bear in mind that it will
always at some level provoke rebellion. Opposition is to be expected.
But we should remember the strange central truth of the Gospel that
sacrifice is more effective than anything else, and witness more important than words.

A homilist should be willing to speak up, ready to give reasons for
one's hope—up to a point (see 1 Pt 3:15). Because, ultimately, one's
trust must lay elsewhere. Trusting in the Cross, which is God's definitive
word, the homilist bears witness by being willing to suffer, understanding
that when meeting the hardened opposition of the world, the preacher
doesn't do so alone. That is, the preacher must have faith in the active
presence of the crucified and risen Christ, present not only in the valley
of the shadow of death but in the pulpit too.

Martin Luther King Jr. experienced such opposition. Early in 1956,
when the young King was first feeling the pressure and threats of the
Montgomery bus boycott, he received a call at home late one Friday

evening. The sinister voice on the end of the line threatened to blow up his family and his home. Bothered deeply, more than when he'd been threatened in the past, he went into his kitchen to think about his family and how he ended up where he was.

Praying, he said, "Lord, I must confess that I'm weak now. I'm faltering. I'm losing my courage." Frightened and alone, it was one of many moments of darkness King experienced throughout his ministry. Yet there in his kitchen he had what can only be described as a mystical experience, one that would strengthen him the rest of his life: "And it seemed at that moment that I could hear an inner voice saying to me, 'Martin Luther, stand up for righteousness. Stand up for justice. Stand up for truth. And lo I will be with you, even until the end of the world.' . . . I heard the voice of Jesus saying still to fight on. He promised never to leave me, never to leave me alone. No never alone. No never alone. He promised never to leave me, never to leave me alone."[21]

"No never alone"—that's a gift given to genuine preachers in such moments: Christ's presence in the acceptance of adversity. And it's the final purification of the preacher, the indwelling of the promised Advocate and the grace of not being alone.

That's what ultimately liberates: the presence of Christ. And it's what gives the preacher strength to preach in a world not altogether benign in its listening. It's also the preacher's measure. Dietrich Bonhoeffer said once, "Those who are still afraid of men have no fear of God, and those how have fear of God have ceased to be afraid of men. All preachers of the gospel will do well to recollect this saying daily."[22] Such godly fear, of course, presumes experience of Christ's presence. To preach genuinely, one must know, fear, and love Christ. To have courage enough to preach by the navigating lights of the Gospel, one must, without prevarication, submit to the eternal sovereignty of the kingdom of God.

"What I'm afraid of is being charged with being afraid." That's how Augustine put it, preaching hard truth to his people.[23] The preacher's final allegiance must be to God's kingdom and none other. Otherwise our preaching will always be something of a sham. To preach with power is to fear nothing more than God, prizing nothing above that truth that is Christ and that is found fully in the Catholic Church. Only this liberates the homilist to preach with strength. Only this, finally, is the source of the preacher's power.

Yet none of this is bravado, the bourgeois *contra mundum* preaching of comfortable, shallow countercultural protest. Calling for strong preaching, I'm not talking about the pettiness of those who are merely social critics, proudly rousing the likeminded while marginalizing others. I'm not talking about those who hammer away at pet issues, arousing a sense of false righteousness with every angry homily. Rather, I'm talking about those who faithfully preach what they believe God is calling them to preach, trusting only in the truth of it. I'm talking about those who speak gently like Christ before all the bemused and powerful of this world, saying only what needs to be said, until they are called finally to imitate the Lamb's silent sacrifice.

These are the final steps on the way of the preacher, the way of criticism becomes the way of sacrifice. They are the steps of the Passion of Christ, which every preacher must walk. The way to Calvary and the tomb, to Galilee and all the nations, to the parish and beyond—the way of the preacher finally just the way of Christ. Otherwise our words are nothing. Our words are either words of offering before the Eucharist or they are simply noise. They're words leading to sacrifice or to the glorification of the self. In each homily stands the preacher and Christ, but it's always Christ's Gospel, never merely the preacher's. Which is why good preaching always risks crucifixion, because Christ's truth is the only truth we're allowed to preach—truth sometimes still hated.

# 8.
# THE PENTECOST
# OF PREACHING

We need a new heart, a new spirit.
—Bishop Kenneth Untener, *Preaching Better*, chap. 1

Such is the heart and way of the preacher: formed in character, habits, understanding, and wisdom. The faithful preacher is also a person of intellect, of communion, of the Church, of prayer and vision. Likewise, the faithful preacher is humble enough to prize the Gospel more than self.

There's glory to preaching, an ever-youthful goodness, joy, and significance we should, from time to time, remember. This is the unique grandeur of preaching. Phillips Brooks, our guide since the beginning, put it best. Preaching is one of the greatest things a person can do:

> There is no career that can compare with it for a moment in the rich and satisfying relations into which it brings a man with his fellow man, in the deep and interesting insight which it gives him into human nature, and in the chance of the best culture for his own character. Its delight never grows old; its interest never wanes; its stimulus is never exhausted. It is different to a man at each period of his life; but if he is the minister he ought to be, there is no age, from the earliest years when he is his people's brother to the late days when he

is like a father to his children on whom he looks down from the pulpit, in which the ministry has not some fresh charm and chance of usefulness to offer the man whose heart is in it. Let us never think of it any other way than this. Let us rejoice with one another that in a world where there are a great many good and happy things for men to do, God has given us the best and happiest, and made us preachers of His truth.[1]

For those called to it, preaching is the best and happiest task one can take up, beyond comparison. If this is how more Catholic preachers saw preaching, then Catholic preaching would quickly and vastly improve, by simply recognizing the glory of it.

But that would still be insufficient, for the human glory of preaching is just that, human—as easily pagan as Christian. Aristotle, at the end of the day, was not a believer, though wise. Whatever one may learn from whomever one may learn it, human wisdom is simply not enough. All the rhetoric in the world is not enough.

So at the end, we should make clear what has been implicit ever since the beginning: that the way of the preacher is also the way of the Holy Spirit, and that the heart of the preacher is the heart set on fire by the Spirit's Pentecost. Human words are of little worth without this fire, of little use as words worthy of God.

It's always been so. Creation was brought about by speech when God spoke light into being (see Gn 1:3). Redemption, however, is brought about by speech *and fire*, ever since, at least, the miracle of the burning bush (see Ex 3:2). From the fire from the altar of the Lord of Hosts, touching and cleansing the mouth of Isaiah; from the fire shut up in the heart and bones of Jeremiah; from the promised baptism of the Holy Spirit and fire; from Christ's wish that the earth was set ablaze already; and ever since Pentecost, the redeeming Word of God has always come with the gift of fire—divine and uncontrollable (see Is 6:6; Jer 20:9; Mt 3:11; Lk 12:49; Acts 2:3).

Hence the inadequacy of everything I've written, and likewise the inadequacy of anything ever written by anyone on preaching. Despite all the books available on the subject, it remains true, as Benedict XVI said, that the renewal of preaching is "more than just a problem to be solved by theology." After all the work done in study and in rhetoric, what's most important remains utterly beyond human achievement. Because God is involved in preaching. In preaching, "a bit of Pentecost comes to pass."[2] After theology and rhetoric, what's left is for the preacher to call down the fire of God.

And this is possible because the fire of the Holy Spirit that came down upon the Church at Pentecost has also come down upon individual believers—poured, as Paul said, into the hearts of the faithful (see Rom 5:5). Although beyond the powers of human achievement, the Holy Spirit nonetheless comes as pure gift, enabling us to call God our Father and his Son, Jesus, our Lord (see Rom 8:15; 1 Cor 12:3). This is the necessary gift of all new life, the *donum* of the Holy Spirit, without which there simply isn't Christian life.

And without which there is also no preaching. As Hans Urs von Balthasar said, "A person can only bear witness before others to the truth of the gospel provided that he himself has received the abiding, inner witness of the Holy Spirit."[3] This is what remains for the renewal of Catholic preaching as well as the renewal of every preacher. This is why the bishops of the United States, at the end of *Fulfilled in Your Hearing*, asked fellow homilists to "breathe in the Spirit of God," because it's the Holy Spirit who enlivens "human words with divine power."[4]

Praying daily for the creative fire of the Holy Spirit, we ought to pray specifically to become better preachers, as deliberately as we pray for vocations. Augustine said that if the Holy Spirit is poured into those handed over to persecution, "why not also in those who are handing Christ over to learners?"[5] If confessors and martyrs receive the Holy Spirit, so do preachers receive the same gift. The preacher "should rely on the presence of the Risen Lord within him as he preaches, a presence guaranteed by the outpouring of the Spirit received at his ordination."[6] Calling down this fire every day, and not just when preparing to preach, we homilists should dare the Holy Spirit to blaze anew, to forge our characters and set our words on fire.

We ought to pray like Philip Neri. One day in 1544, alone among the catacombs, constantly begging the Holy Spirit for gifts and graces, he got what he prayed for: "He suddenly felt himself divinely filled with the power of the Holy Spirit with such force that his heart began to palpitate within his body and to be inflamed with such love that, his nature being unaccustomed to such a palpitation of the heart, he indicated that he was completely unable to bear it." Filled with the fire of God (many said literally), Neri cried, "Enough, Lord, enough! I cannot take any more!"[7] A mysterious personal pentecost, it changed him forever. Close friends said of him, "His heart glows and emits flames and sparks, so that the passages of his throat are burned as though by a real fire."[8]

Philip Neri spoke with a strange, disconcerting joy, inspiring a new and better sort of preaching. Always speaking "in Spirit and truth and simplicity of heart," he preached with a familiarity and joy that attracted souls, that met listeners where they were with love and sympathy and hope.[9] In a dark age of corruption and sterility, reformation and renewal, he introduced a new way of preaching that changed the Church, all because he begged for the Holy Spirit and let his heart catch flame.

No less today, we need homilists to beg the Holy Spirit for a new pentecost of preaching. Whatever I or anyone else writes about homiletics, only this will bring about the renewal of Catholic preaching. It's prayer to the Holy Spirit that belongs to the greater renewal of the Church, the renewal of the fledgling and the lapsed, of even unbelievers and the world.

We need the Holy Spirit's fire afresh. Ours is a world no longer of benign doubt or disbelief. Ours is no longer a Church that can rest upon its cultural heritage. Unbelievers outside the Church and in, doubters and strugglers in our pews and on the margins: too many hear homilies that simply do not move them. Too often, Sunday by Sunday, they hear preaching that is shallow and trite, poorly thought out and poorly delivered. Too often they hear preaching that's spiritless and heartless. Innumerable souls never see what God wants them to see—himself in the breaking of the bread—in no small part because our preaching is not worthy of either God or his people. Because it's lifeless, heartless, fireless.

Each preacher should pray the prayer of the Psalmist: "Let those who seek you, God of Israel, not be disgraced because of me" (Ps 69:7). We homilists must understand our role in the lives of those who listen to us preach. "And how can they hear without someone to preach?" Paul asked (Rom 10:14). We must grasp the serious responsibility of preaching, bearing in mind the judgment God still promises his preachers. We must realize how, in a profound reality, God is spoken by our lips and taken into the ears and hearts of those who listen. And we must care how easily we can ruin that grace by our negligence, letting God go unheard through our own most grievous fault.

The renewal of Catholic preaching demands that we realize preaching is indeed that important. We must let go of that pseudo-Catholic assumption that we needn't care that much about preaching, just because we're a sacramental Church. Taking scripture seriously, we must listen to the teaching of genuine Catholic tradition and understand that preaching bears an importance unrivaled alongside all the sacraments of the Church.

The Church needs better preachers, the world too. The renewal of the whole Church awaits the renewal of preaching, renewal awaiting homilists deeply formed and who speak from the heart. If the Church is to stand well against the many hopeless ideologies of secular modernity, if the Church is to save those lost to the faith as well as strengthen those who are struggling, then the Church's preachers must have a good word, fully human and divine. In a world of bitter noise, ours must be a beautiful word of love. In a world in which so many are seeking what they don't even know, ours must be words of light. They must be words not only of truth but also of beauty.

To preach as we must in this darkening age of shrinking faith, if we're to be heralds of dawn at dusk, we need the Holy Spirit with all its cataclysmic, redeeming power. We need the Spirit to shake our Church and set it ablaze. And we need our preachers lit ablaze, too, because nothing but "fire kindles fire."[10]

Hence the heart and way of the preacher. Hence the urgency. Hence prayer, begging the Holy Spirit to come down anew. Hence our prayer that preachers breathe in fire. Hence this new pentecost of preaching. Shakespeare prayed, and for a mere play, "O, for a muse of fire that would ascend / The brightest heaven of invention!"[11] Our prayer, however, is for a more lasting work and more sacred art: preaching the Gospel of Christ and the kingdom of God.

This is the work of words of divine fire, spoken by us.

# EPILOGUE: THE WAY OF THE LISTENER

What are we to do, my brothers and sisters?

—see Acts 2:37

The Church is clear. Listening to a homily is not a passive experience. A homily is dialogue, not monologue. Listeners are active participants in what is primarily a dialogue between God and his people, a dialogue in which the preacher stands not as gatekeeper or oracle but as mediator, as ordained minister sharing in the common priesthood of brothers and sisters as they both hear and respond to God in love.

Augustine, for example, often rhetorically placed himself beside his congregation as if all of them together had turned toward God. He would often say to his congregation things such as, "Don't listen to me, but together with me," and, "Let's be companions in believing . . . companions in seeking."[1] Pope Francis likened homilies to the sort of talk that goes on in families, as "a mother speaks to her child." But he didn't mean by this image to suggest that listeners are passive; rather, he was clear that all people, whatever their state in life, are "agents of evangelization" (*Evangelii Gaudium*, 139, 120). That is, in the event of the Gospel's proclamation, in preaching, both laity and clergy are active participants in equal measure.

And the purpose of this dialogue between God and preacher and people is twofold. It's to bring about union with Christ by faith and by sacrament, but then to send us out into the world as friends and servants and even potentially as martyrs of Christ. The purpose is to become what Francis called "missionary disciples" (*Evangelii Gaudium*, 120).

The first goal of preaching is to set hearts aflame with desire for Christ, just as the hearts of those two wandering disciples burned when they heard the risen Lord talk about the scriptures. It's to bring listeners to ask Jesus, as they did, "Stay with us," and then to lead them to that moment when they will recognize the Lord in the breaking of the bread (Lk 24:29–32).

But then quickly the goal becomes mission—for listeners to become, in a sense, preachers themselves. "Go and announce the Gospel of the Lord," the deacon says at the end of the Mass.[2] Like Jesus at his baptism, declared from heaven the Father's "beloved Son" and then sent into the desert by the Spirit, so too are Christians inspired and drawn close to Christ in word and sacrament and then driven out into the world by the same Spirit (Mk 1:11–12).

Good preaching should always provoke listeners to ask some form of this question: "What are we to do?" It's the question posed by those first hearers of the first sermon of the apostolic era after Peter, filled with the Pentecost Spirit, preached the risen Christ, leaving his listeners "cut to the heart"(Acts 2:37). A good homily brings listeners to a moment of crisis, conversion, and conviction. That is, a homily should nudge, inspire, move, and persuade. Or, as Augustine put it, the point of preaching is to "conquer and win them."[3]

In this, Christian preaching is no different from other forms of rhetoric, which is why Church Fathers and theologians for centuries have been able to make use of Cicero and Aristotle and other great teachers of the art. But what's different about Christian preaching is that, unlike other rhetorical endeavors, it can usher listeners into the life and mission of God himself. The homily is sacramental in this sense, because it prepares us for an encounter with the Lord.

That's why every person who comes to Mass should prepare themselves. It is painfully evident that clergy need to do a lot of work to improve the quality of their preaching. However, the laity also need to do a lot of work to improve the quality of their listening. We should not complain about bad preaching if we do nothing on our part to hear well the Word of God offered by the preacher. If preaching is to improve, then both clergy and laity must work together. Plutarch, millennia ago, said that speaking and listening ought to be learned together. He said it's like playing ball; "learning to throw and learning to catch take place at the same time."[4] This is true for the dialogue of preaching. We're Church, not theater. We're pilgrims together in dialogue, not a schoolhouse of teachers lecturing silent students.

So here are some steps for the listener. When embraced as a spiritual rule, these steps are meant to allow listeners to get the most out of homilies, even bad ones. Since we're all called to be active listeners and pilgrims, and since the homily belongs to the great dialogue between God and humanity as well as to mission, each of us has a responsibility to engage the event of preaching intentionally, giving the Word of God and the preacher our best. That's what these steps are meant to achieve.

# Step 1: Read the Lectionary in Advance

The dogmatic constitution *Dei Verbum* from the Second Vatican Council teaches that a homily "should be nourished and ruled by sacred Scripture" (*Dei Verbum*, 21). That is, the very essence of any homily should be biblical. The reason for this, of course, is that the Word of God best sets the heart aflame with desire for union with Christ. A lecture may give you information about Jesus of Nazareth or about an ancient text, but a homily is sacramental. It prepares you for an encounter, not an exam.

Thus, the first thing any serious listener of homilies should do is read the Lectionary, the biblical readings appointed for the upcoming Sunday Mass. It's best to do this several days in advance at least, allowing time for meditation, study, and prayer. Pope Francis argued that when preparing for homilies, preachers "need to be sure that we understand the meaning of the *words* we read." The Lectionary comprises ancient biblical texts that demand some level of study, so the preacher must make the effort to "discover the principle message" of the passages appointed (*Evangelii Gaudium*, 147). But if this is true for preachers, it's also true for listeners. Again, it's not the purpose of the homily for the preacher to do all the work to supply passive hearers with information. Both preacher and congregation are meant to encounter the Word of God together.

And for this, Benedict XVI recommended lectio divina not only for homilists, who in prayer and meditation must "be in close and constant contact with the sacred text," but also for the laity (*Verbum Domini*, 59). And that's because of the deep relationship between scripture and the Eucharist. Reading and meditating on scripture, just as it did for those two disciples on the road to Emmaus, "prepares for, accompanies, and deepens what the Church celebrates when she proclaims the word in a liturgical setting" (*Verbum Domini*, 86). That is, reading scripture will always open our hearts to experience the Mass more deeply. It's like rereading your favorite book before seeing the movie or listening to an album by your favorite band before seeing them in concert. But it's even more enriching than this because it's the Word of God.

Thus, before even sitting down in a pew on Sunday morning, we already ought to be listeners of the Word of God, our hearts and minds ready for whatever the preached Word will be.

# Step 2: Pray for Your Preachers

The Bible is full of warnings for preachers, which is probably why it's also full of people trying to wriggle out of God's call. Moses tried to excuse himself because of a speech impediment, Jeremiah because of his youth, while Jonah just up and ran away (see Ex 4:10; Jer 1:6; Jon 1:3). And that's because serving as a mouthpiece for God is demanding, often requiring great sacrifice.

Paul spoke of it in terms of an "obligation" laid upon him. "Woe to me if I do not preach it!" he wrote to the Corinthians (1 Cor 9:16). He knew well the tension that sometimes exists between preacher and people—for instance, when he asked the Galatians, "Have I become your enemy by telling you the truth?" (Gal 4:16). John Chrysostom, who supposedly tried to evade ordination, explained to his friend Basil, "I am afraid that if I receive the flock from Christ plump and well fed and then damage it through ineptitude I may provoke against me God."[5]

Risking either the hostility of the people or the final judgment of God, homilists face an often very frightening task. For that reason alone, we should pray for preachers. Because they've put themselves under both the judgment of God and the scrutiny of the people for the sake of truth and the salvation of souls.

But more importantly, we should pray for preachers for the sake of communion and mission. When we commit to reading the Lectionary in advance of the Sunday liturgy, we're already in a special sort of communion with our preacher, who has undoubtedly been meditating upon the same texts under the guidance of the same Spirit. And that can only bear fruit as both the laity and the preacher share in the great dialogue between God and his people. Prayer increases the bonds of charity among believers. Between preacher and congregation this translates into sympathy and into a better understanding of God's will for each of us and for the Church.

# Step 3: Expect the Holy Spirit to Speak

Always remember, there is no biblical account of the ascension of the Holy Spirit. As St. Óscar Romero said once, "It will always be Pentecost in the church."[6] John's gospel records Jesus' promise of the Holy Spirit, which will lead disciples to conviction and truth (see Jn 16:8–13). The gift of Pentecost, this Spirit, continues to dwell in us (see Rom 8:9).

And it's a Spirit involved in words and speech, charismatically in the moment. Jesus promised the Holy Spirit to those suffering persecutions, saying that the Spirit would speak through them (see Mk 13:11). To speak wisdom and knowledge are gifts of the Spirit (see 1 Cor 12:8). The Spirit, as Paul testified, accompanied his words with divine power. Even when his words were weak, the Spirit still flowed through them (see 1 Cor 1:4–5).

All of this suggests that when we listen to a homily, we should believe that the Holy Spirit is present and active. We should expect the Holy Spirit to speak. Even if it's a poorly delivered homily, the Holy Spirit is still at work. "Some of the best things I have ever thought of I have thought of during bad sermons," said Jayber in Wendell Berry's novel,

*Jayber Crow.*[7] Even in bad preaching, Christ is still present, able to change lives because of the gift of Pentecost. Thus, each of us must simply do our best not to stifle the Spirit (see 1 Thes 5:19).

# Step 4: Struggle to Listen

In the *Rule for a New Brother*, the beautiful rule of life written for the community of the Congregation of the Blessed Sacrament in Brakkenstein, Holland, there's a part that reads, "Let yourself be renewed in your faith, hope and love by the Word that comes to you. Don't let yourself be distracted by accidentals. Try to understand God's Word even in the mouth of a bad reader."[8] It's a simple reminder that the Holy Spirit is present in faithful words, even if poorly spoken.

It would be great, of course, if every reader and every preacher's every word were heard perfectly by everyone, if sound systems never let us down and accents never bothered us. But that's not reality. What's reality is that sometimes the homily is very hard to hear. Maybe there's a baby crying right behind us, or maybe the homilist's first language isn't our own, or maybe we found the one spot in the Church the speakers don't reach. It happens to everyone. Sometimes we just can't hear a thing.

But that doesn't mean our experience of the homily is ruined. Rather, it just means we have a new spiritual opportunity. It's like the parable of the sower, the seed fallen on the path symbolizing the person "who hears the word of the kingdom without understanding it" (Mt 13:19). Instead of pulling out our phone or getting upset, what we should do in that moment is pray for ears to hear, as Jesus said (see Mt 13:9, 19). In those moments when it's hard to hear the preacher, we should be like the merchant in search of the "pearl of great price" or the woman in search of her lost coin (see Mt 13:44–46; Lk 15:8–10).

Literally, we should lean in, close our eyes, and make every effort to glean some word, some wisdom from the Lord. Even if the preacher is a poor speaker, even if the homily itself isn't all that great, the Holy Spirit is nonetheless present and nonetheless powerful, so it's still worth the struggle to listen. At the very least, our struggle to hear the Gospel will itself become a prayer of desire for the Word of God. And that's not a prayer that will long go unanswered.

# Step 5: Don't Complain about the Length of the Homily

It can be dangerous for homilies to go on too long. Just ask Eutychus. As Paul "talked on and on" until midnight, he was the young man who fell asleep and then three stories to his death, all because the sermon went on a bit too long (see Acts 20:7–9). Sometimes preachers do get a little overzealous. James Davenport, for example, perhaps the most radical preacher of the Great Awakening, once tried to preach a full twenty-four hours without stopping—collapsing after a while, blessedly.[9] Indeed, sometimes preachers do go too long. It happens to the best of us. Even apostles, even popes, even bishops, even parish priests: sometimes we do indeed go on more than we should.

Pope Francis taught that although a preacher should be able "to hold the attention of his listeners for a whole hour," of course one shouldn't. He said this not because of any theories about declining attention spans but because of the principle that the homily should always serve the liturgy and not the other way around (*Evangelii Gaudium*, 138).

Nonetheless, there is no ideal length for homilies, not even really a rule of thumb. And that's the way it should be. Aristotle taught that a person should speak "just as much as will make the thing clear."[10] In a homily, since the Holy Spirit is involved, it's up to the Spirit how long the homily should be. Our job is simply to resist the temptation to put a stopwatch on God.

So for both preacher and people, that means focusing on focusing. The preacher should focus on God and simply strive to be faithful to what God wants to say, no matter the length. The people, in turn, should focus as well, remembering they're servants who do not own the time they're worrying about. Because again, this is the Word of God we're talking about—not ordinary speech, but a divine word with the power to change lives. It's a word worth waiting for.

# Step 6: Listen for What Inspires You

The Word of God, by its very nature, inspires. Or, as Paul said, the Word of God "can build you up" (Acts 20:32). And that's because the Word of God is creative and redemptive, the "mighty word" that "sustains all things" (Heb 1:3).

But it's also a personal word, the word of the Shepherd who loves his sheep and knows them by name (see Jn 10:4). Thus, just as the risen Lord spoke personally to Mary Magdalene as she sat weeping in the darkness, so it's possible that through the homily, some personal word of inspiration might be meant for each of us (see Jn 20:16). We must simply be content to wait and wonder and listen for it.

If we believe the Holy Spirit to be present and active in the homily, and if we've given ourselves and our time wholly to the Lord, then it's reasonable to expect the Lord to speak. It's reasonable to expect that just as he wrestled with Jacob, whispered to Samuel, called Mary Magdalene by name, and knocked Paul off his horse, so too may he do the same to us.

But again, it depends on whether we approach the homily either as a spiritual opportunity or as a burden upon our time.

# Step 7: Listen for What Upsets You

If you've never been upset by a homily, it may be that you've never heard the Gospel. Augustine tells of an experience preaching in Caesarea of Mauritania in modern-day Algeria, a town riven by ritual violence. Preaching there, and of course trying to put an end to such nonsense, Augustine said, "I did not consider I had achieved anything when I heard them applauding me, but only when I saw them weeping."[11] And that's because tears meant change.

It is quite simply part of the tradition and part of the preacher's responsibility to proclaim the entire Gospel, even when it hurts. Preaching in Nazareth at the beginning of his public ministry, Jesus enraged his listeners. They were "filled with fury," Luke says, so much that they tried to throw Jesus off a cliff (Lk 4:28–30). Stephen called his listeners "stiff-necked people," which, of course, infuriated them, bringing about the first martyrdom of the Christian age (Acts 7:51–60).

Provocative and even irritating preaching belongs to the prophetic character of the Church. It always has. Read the sermons on the poor by John Chrysostom or the Cappadocians in the fourth century. Read the sermons of St. John Vianney; his first sermon in Ars, he said, "I weep over you. . . . Hell exists."[12] Read Pope Francis! Preaching that upsets is often preaching that's genuine. Often it's the very preaching filled with the Spirit, which, as Jesus said, would be a Spirit of conviction (see Jn 16:8–11).

Of course, as Pope Francis said, good preaching "does not leave us trapped in negativity"; rather, it always offers hope (*Evangelii Gaudium*, 159). With genuine preaching, there is always deep, genuine joy, always a path open for listeners leading from darkness to light. Yet it still may pack a punch, still sting. And that's because the Gospel calls us to repentance, which is sometimes an unwelcome message.

But that's also why we should listen for what upsets us, but without getting offended. Because often what upsets us is precisely what God wants us to think about and reconsider. And so, if we're mature Christians and mature hearers of the Gospel, we should be mature enough to hear hard preaching. Otherwise we shouldn't bother listening at all.

# Step 8: Seek the Call to Obedience and Action

All rhetoric is meant to be persuasive. Its purpose is to change minds, inspire action. In Christianity, we call this "the obedience of faith" (Rom 1:5; 16:26). And it's the final ethical fruit of all good preaching.

Of course, obedience isn't particularly popular. Today especially, ours is an age of consumer independence, ubiquitous choice, changing the channel. With our modern idea of freedom as simply freedom for freedom's sake, it's hard for us to make sense of obedience, much less put it into practice.

Yet that doesn't change the fact that we need obedience. Simone Weil called obedience "a vital need of the human soul." Without it, she said, we're ill.[13] And she was right.

That's why, when listening to a homily, we should seek the call to obedience. After a homily, we should always ask ourselves some form of that first question asked after Peter's first homily, "What are we to do, my brothers?" (Acts 2:37). It's a question meant for the perfecting of faith—giving faith, as Thomas Aquinas taught, the form of charity.[14]

That is, if the homily belongs to the liturgy and the Holy Spirit, then it belongs to the work of redemption and to action, both upon the altar and in the world. That is to say, the homily and the Eucharist should come together to bring us to a deeper, more committed Christian love. However, it isn't magic. It can only happen by means of obedience.

# Step 9: Talk about the Homily Afterward

If the Holy Spirit, which dwells within us, is also the Spirit of truth capable of guiding us into "all truth" as Jesus said, and if it's true that where two or three are gathered in his name, he is present, then it's reasonable to suggest that when Christians come together in conversation and dialogue, it is a spiritual opportunity to say the least (see Jn 16:13; Mt 18:20; Rom 8:9). At the beginning of St. Aelred of Rievaulx's *Spiritual Friendship*, he writes, "Here we are, you and I, and I hope a third, Christ in our midst."[15] Such is the gift of belonging within the Communion of Saints. Between us is always more, always the Spirit and always Christ, in union with the Father.

This means that when Christians come together to talk about the Word of God, there's always more to that too. Gregory the Great said that often he couldn't understand scripture until he placed himself in the midst of his community.[16] That is why the Church continually calls upon all of us to take up study of the Bible. As Pope Francis said, "Study of sacred Scripture must be a door opened to every believer" (*Evangelii Gaudium*, 175). Because when Christians talk together about the Bible, God talks too.

And this is true for homilies as well. That first question from that first homily in the Acts of the Apostles—"What are we to do, my brothers?"—was a communal question, a question asked by the men and women present together (Acts 2:37). Dialogue belongs to the nature of the homily.

Talking with family or friends about the homily after Mass can be a spiritual exercise, a moment of communion. In the car, or at breakfast or lunch, casual conversation can turn into something sacramental. Journaling, being in conversation with oneself and the Spirit, is a good idea too. In these ways not only can we gather something we may have missed, some insight we didn't consider before, but we can also grow closer to our fellow listeners as fellow disciples.

# Step 10: Remember the Homily Later in the Week

This last step is simple, but no less important. A few days or so after the homily, and before reading the Lectionary for the next Sunday and beginning this process all over again, we should think about the previous homily. We should call to mind whatever keynote, fruit, or consolation we gained.

The various selections from the Lectionary and the liturgical texts and homilies that are offered Sunday by Sunday do not exist in isolation from one another. Rather, they exist in liturgical time, speaking together as a living voice in the present. Geoffrey Wainwright, the Methodist theologian, called this the "hermeneutical continuum," by which he meant very simply that when scripture is read within the ongoing context of the liturgy, then biblical interpretation, theology, and doctrine all function as they should, presenting most clearly within the act of worship the revelation of the living Christ.[17]

This means that if we take up the practice of reading the Lectionary, listening and reflecting upon the homily (even if poorly thought out or delivered), doing this week in and week out, then we will be better able to listen to what the Lord is saying to each of us and to the Church *today*. The ancient word becomes the contemporary word, and the whole experience of weekly worship becomes dialogue and an experience of invitation, response, and love.

# We Must Improve Together

We preachers must acknowledge the crisis of bad preaching, accept our part in it, and take real steps to improve this part of our ministry. The time for this was yesterday. But the laity ought to assume responsibility in this crisis too. That's what the way of the listener is about.

The preached Gospel, as Paul said, "is not of human origin" (Gal 1:11). Yet homilies can still be awful. Nonetheless, God ordains frail humans to be his preachers, because it is the human voice that sometimes best speaks God's love, as strange as that sounds. The job of each of us and all of us together, therefore, is to offer God and his Gospel our best, which means offering our preachers and the homilies we experience our best too.

We preachers should strive to preach well, which is what this book has been about. But in return, laypeople can try to become better hearers of the Gospel. That's an important matter, too, because preaching simply won't improve without better listeners as well as better preachers.

Because we're all equally the Church, missionary disciples together, tasked with speaking the Gospel to our world.

# NOTES

## Preface

1. Timothy Radcliffe, introduction to *A Handbook for Catholic Preaching*, ed. Edward Foley (Collegeville, MN: Liturgical Press, 2016), xi.

2. Hughes Oliphant Old, *The Reading and Preaching of the Scriptures in the Worship of the Christian Church*, 1:2 (Grand Rapids, MI: Wm. B. Eerdmans Publishing Co., 1998).

3. "Kendrick Lamar Thinks Preaching Has Gotten Too Watered Down," *Relevant Magazine*, May 1, 2017, https://relevantmagazine.com/slice/kendrick-lamar-thinks-preaching-has-gotten-too-watered-down.

4. Martin Luther King Jr., "Letter from a Birmingham Jail," in Jonathan Rieder, *Gospel of Freedom: Martin Luther King, Jr.'s Letter from Birmingham Jail and the Struggle That Changed a Nation* (New York: Bloomsbury Press, 2014), 182.

5. Dante Alighieri, *Paradiso*, trans. Robert Hollander and Jean Hollander (New York: Anchor Books, 2007), canto 29, 94–110.

6. Mark Thompson, *Enough Said: What's Gone Wrong with the Language of Politics?* (New York: St. Martin's Press, 2017), 18, 74.

7. Charles Taylor, *A Secular Age* (Cambridge, MA: Belknap Press of Harvard University Press, 2007), 551.

8. Johann Hari, *Lost Connections: Uncovering the Real Causes of Depression—and the Unexpected Solutions* (New York: Bloomsbury Press, 2017).

9. Plato, *Gorgias*, trans. Donald J. Zeyl (Indianapolis: Hackett, 1987), 504d.

10. Michel de Certeau, *The Practice of Everyday Life* (Berkeley: University of California Press, 1988), 43.

11. Ian Ker, *John Henry Newman* (Oxford: Oxford University Press, 1990), 19.

12. John Chrysostom, *Six Books on the Priesthood*, trans. Graham Neville (Yonkers, NY: St. Vladimir's Seminary Press, 1996), 5.1.

13. *Homiletic Directory* (Vatican City: Libreria Editrice Vaticana, 2014), see 4.

# Part I: Redeeming the Heart of the Preacher

1. James Mallon, *Divine Renovation: Bringing Your Parish from Maintenance to Mission* (New London, CT: Twenty-Third Publications, 2014), 129.

2. Plato, *Phaedrus*, trans. Stephen Scully (Newburyport, MA: Focus, 2003), 261a8.

3. Yves Congar, *At the Heart of Christian Worship: Liturgical Essays of Yves Congar* (Collegeville, MN: Liturgical Press, 2010), 10.

4. Hans Urs von Balthasar, *Explorations in Theology* II (San Francisco: Ignatius Press, 1991), 395.

5. Aristotle, *On Rhetoric: A Theory of Civic Discourse*, trans. George A. Kennedy (Oxford: Oxford University Press, 2007), 1356a.

6. Isocrates, *Isocrates*, trans. George Norlin (Cambridge, MA: Harvard University Press, 2006), 14.

7. Aristotle, *Nicomachean Ethics*, trans. Terence Irwin (Indianapolis: Hackett, 2007), 1103a.

8. Raymond E. Brown, *The Gospel According to John*, vol. 29 (Garden City, NY: Anchor Bible, 1966), 320–23.

9. Bernard of Clairvaux, *Sermons on Conversion*, trans. Marie-Bernard Saïd (Kalamazoo, MI: Cistercian Publications, 1981).

10. Phillips Brooks, *The Joy of Preaching* (Grand Rapids, MI: Kregel Publications, 1989), 26–27.

11. Aristotle, *On Rhetoric*, 1378a.

12. Brooks, *Joy of Preaching*, 29.

13. Karla Bellinger, *Connecting Pulpit and Pew: Breaking Open the Conversation about Catholic Preaching* (Collegeville, MN: Liturgical Press, 2014), 30.

14. Fred B. Craddock, *Preaching* (Nashville: Abingdon Press, 1997), 24.

15. *Fulfilled in Your Hearing: The Homily in the Sunday Assembly* (Washington, DC: United States Catholic Conference, 1982), 7–8.

16. Craddock, *Preaching*, 24.

17. Thomas S. Kidd, *The Great Awakening* (New Haven, CT: Yale University Press, 2007), 48.

# 1. The Preacher as Public Intellectual

1. Cicero, *On Invention*, in *Cicero*, vol. 1, trans. Harry Mortimer Hubbell (Cambridge, MA: Harvard University Press, 1949), 1.1.

2. Augustine, *Teaching Christianity*, trans. Edmund Hill (Hyde Park, NY: New City Press, 2013), 4.7.21.

3. Augustine, *Teaching Christianity*, 4.15.32. See also Cicero, *The Orator*, in *Cicero*, vol. 5, trans. G. L. Hendrickson and Harry Mortimer Hubbell (Cambridge, MA: Harvard University Press, 1971), 21.69.

4. Humbert of Romans, *Treatise on the Formation of Preachers*, in *Early Dominicans: Selected Writings*, ed. Simon Tugwell (New York: Paulist Press, 1982), 82.

5. *The Rites of the Catholic Church* (Collegeville, MN: Liturgical Press, 1991), 15, emphasis added.

6. Hannah Arendt, *Between Past and Future* (London: Penguin, 2006), 91.

7. Dietrich Bonhoeffer, *Ethics*, trans. Eberhard Bethge (New York: Macmillan, 1965), 114.

8. *The Priest and the Third Christian Millennium: Teacher of the Word, Minister of the Sacraments, and Leader of the Community* (Washington, DC: United States Catholic Conference, 1999), 2.2.

9. Plato, *Theaetetus*, trans. M. J. Levett (Indianapolis: Hackett, 1999), 155c–d.

10. Václav Havel, *The Art of the Impossible: Politics as Morality in Practice: Speeches and Writings, 1990–1996* (New York: Knopf, 1997), 207.

11. Havel, *Art of the Impossible*, 185.

12. Aleksandr Isaevich Solzhenitsyn, *The Nobel Lecture on Literature*, trans. Thomas P. Whitney (New York: Harper and Row, 1972), 37.

13. Joseph W. Trigg, *Origen* (London: Routledge, 2004), 211; Augustine, *Teaching Christianity*, 2.18.28; Martin Luther King Jr., *Strength to Love* (Philadelphia: Fortress, 1981), 51; Robert Barron, *Seeds of the Word: Finding God in the Culture* (Skokie, IL: Word on Fire, 2015).

14. Kevin J. Vanhoozer and Owen Strachan, *The Pastor as Public Theologian: Reclaiming a Lost Vision* (Grand Rapids, MI: Baker Academic, 2015), 9.

15. Vanhoozer and Strachan, *Pastor as Public Theologian*, 15.

16. Vanhoozer and Strachan, *Pastor as Public Theologian*, 23.

17. Vanhoozer and Strachan, *Pastor as Public Theologian*, 27.

18. Thomas G. Long, *The Witness of Preaching* (Louisville, KY: Westminster John Knox Press, 2005), 223.

19. John Chrysostom, *Six Books on the Priesthood*, trans. Graham Neville (Yonkers, NY: St. Vladimir's Seminary Press, 1996), 4.3.

20. Henry David Thoreau, *A Week on the Concord and Merrimack Rivers* (London: Penguin, 2000), 77.

21. Fred B. Craddock, *Preaching* (Nashville: Abingdon Press, 1997), 70.

22. Phillips Brooks, *The Joy of Preaching* (Grand Rapids, MI: Kregel Publications, 1989), 107.

23. John Henry Newman, *The Idea of a University* (Notre Dame, IN: University of Notre Dame Press, 2003), 101.

24. Wendell Berry, *Citizenship Papers: Essays* (Oxford: Basic Books, 2004), 21.

25. John Paul II, *Gift and Mystery* (New York: Doubleday, 1996), 92.

26. Albert Camus, *Resistance, Rebellion, and Death* (New York: Modern Library, 1960), 48.

## 2. The Communion of Preachers

1. Augustine, *Teaching Christianity*, trans. Edmund Hill (Hyde Park, NY: New City Press, 2013), 4.2.3.

2. Augustine, *Teaching Christianity*, 4.3.4.

3. Augustine, *Teaching Christianity*, 4.5.8.

4. Plato, *Phaedrus* (New York: Arno Press, 1973), 261b.

5. Cicero, *On Invention*, in *Cicero*, vol. 1, trans. Harry Mortimer Hubbell (Cambridge, MA: Harvard University Press, 1949), 1.1.

6. Aristotle, *On Rhetoric: A Theory of Civic Discourse*, trans. George A. Kennedy (Oxford: Oxford University Press, 2007), 1355a.

7. Aristotle, *On Rhetoric*, 1356a.

8. John Chrysostom, *Six Books on the Priest Lord*, trans. Graham Neville (Yonkers, NY: St. Vladimir's Seminary Press, 1996), 4.6.

9. Augustine, *Teaching Christianity*, 4.5.7, 4.10.25.

10. Aristotle, *Nicomachean Ethics*, trans. Terence Irwin (Indianapolis: Hackett, 2007), 1103a–1103b.

11. Fred B. Craddock, *Preaching* (Nashville: Abingdon Press, 1997), 204.

12. Martin Luther King Jr., *A Knock at Midnight: Inspiration from the Great Sermons of Reverend Martin Luther King, Jr.* (New York: Intellectual Properties Management in association with Warner Books, 2000), 108.

13. King, *Knock at Midnight*, 108.

14. Martin Luther King Jr., "Letter from a Birmingham Jail," in Jonathan Rieder, *Gospel of Freedom: Martin Luther King, Jr.'s Letter from Birmingham Jail and the Struggle That Changed a Nation* (New York: Bloomsbury Press, 2014), 180.

15. Winston S. Churchill, *Blood, Toil, Tears and Sweat: The Speeches of Winston Churchill* (London: Cassell, 1997), 149.

16. Dante Alighieri, *Paradiso*, trans. Robert Hollander and Jean Hollander (New York: Anchor Books, 2007), canto 10, 94–96.

17. Karla Bellinger, *Connecting Pulpit and Pew: Breaking Open the Conversation about Catholic Preaching* (Collegeville, MN: Liturgical Press, 2014), 45.

18. Craddock, *Preaching*, 37.

19. Augustine, *The City of God: Against the Pagans*, trans. Henry Bettenson (Middlesex, UK: Penguin, 1984), 22.29.

20. Joseph Ratzinger, *Church, Ecumenism, and Politics: New Essays in Ecclesiology* (Slough, UK: St. Paul Publications, 1988), 34–36.

21. Phillips Brooks, *The Joy of Preaching* (Grand Rapids, MI: Kregel Publications, 1989), 26.

# 3. The Preacher and the Fullness of the Church

1. Irenaeus, *Against Heresies*, in Robert M. Grant, *Irenaeus of Lyons* (London: Routledge, 2003), 1.10.2.

2. Irenaeus, *Against Heresies*, 1.10.2.

3. Irenaeus, *Against Heresies*, 1.10.2

4. Irenaeus, *Against Heresies*, 3.4.1.

5. Augustine, *Teaching Christianity*, trans. Edmund Hill (Hyde Park, NY: New City Press, 2013), 3.15.23, 3.2.2.

6. Basil the Great, *On the Holy Spirit* (Yonkers, NY: St. Vladimir's Seminary Press, 2007), 27.66.

7. Benedict XVI, *Dogma and Preaching: Applying Christian Doctrine to Daily Life*, trans. Michael J. Miller and Matthew J. O'Connell (San Francisco: Ignatius Press, 2011), 15.

8. Benedict XVI, *Dogma and Preaching*, 34.

9. Raymond Studzinski, *Reading to Live: The Evolving Practice of Lectio Divina* (Trappist, KY: Cistercian Publications, 2009), 130.

10. Benedict XVI, *Dogma and Preaching*, 21.

11. Simone Weil, *The Need for Roots: Prelude to a Declaration of Duties towards Mankind*, trans. Arthur Wills (London: Routledge, 2010), 14.

12. Gregory of Nazianzus, *Oration*, in *St. Gregory of Nazianzus: Select Orations*, trans. Martha Vinson (Washington, DC: Catholic University of America Press, 2003), 22.6–8.

13. Phillips Brooks, *The Joy of Preaching* (Grand Rapids, MI: Kregel Publications, 1989), 25.

14. Yves Congar, *True and False Reform in the Church*, trans. Paul Philibert (Collegeville, MN: Liturgical Press, 2011), 190.

15. Jean-Pierre Torrell, *Saint Thomas Aquinas*, vol. 1, trans. Robert Royal (Washington, DC: Catholic University of America Press, 2005), 293.

16. Congar, *True and False Reform in the Church*, 189.

17. Wendell Berry, *Jayber Crow* (Washington, DC: Counterpoint, 2000), 160.

18. Carol Harrison, *The Art of Listening in the Early Church* (Oxford: Oxford University Press, 2015), 143.

19. Thomas G. Long, *The Witness of Preaching* (Louisville, KY: Westminster John Knox Press, 2005), 18–51.

20. Brooks, *Joy of Preaching*, 130.

21. Fred B. Craddock, *Preaching* (Nashville: Abingdon Press, 1997), 95, emphasis original.

22. Richard H. Thaler and Cass R. Sunstein, *Nudge: Improving Decisions about Health, Wealth, and Happiness* (New York: Penguin, 2009), 5.

23. Gregory the Great, *Pastoral Care* (New York: Newman Press, 1978), 3, prologue.

24. Sarah Bernhardt, *My Double Life: Memoirs of Sarah Bernhardt* (London: William Heinemann, 1907), 402.

25. Augustine, *Letter* 95.2, in *A Select Library of the Nicene and Post-Nicene Fathers of the Christian Church, 1st ser.*, ed. Alexander Roberts, James Donaldson, Philip Schaff, and Henry Wace (Edinburgh: T and T Clark, 1996).

26. Yves Congar, *Lay People in the Church: A Study for a Theology of Laity* (London: G. Chapman, 1985), 294.

27. Maurice Friedman, *Encounter on the Narrow Ridge: A Life of Martin Buber* (New York: Paragon House, 1993), 126.

28. Brooks, *Joy of Preaching*, 26.

29. Henri de Lubac, *The Splendor of the Church* (San Francisco: Ignatius Press, 1999), 240–41.

30. de Lubac, *Splendor of the Church*, 258.

31. de Lubac, *Splendor of the Church*, 264.

# Part II: Redeeming the Way of the Preacher

1. Plato, *Gorgias*, trans. Donald J. Zeyl (Indianapolis: Hackett, 1987), 462b–66a.

2. Aristotle, *On Rhetoric: A Theory of Civic Discourse*, trans. George A. Kennedy (Oxford: Oxford University Press, 2007), 1354a; *Nicomachean Ethics*, trans. Terence Irwin (Indianapolis: Hackett, 2007), 1140a.

3. Aristotle, *On Rhetoric*, 1354a–1355b.

4. Augustine, *Teaching Christianity*, trans. Edmund Hill (Hyde Park, NY: New City Press, 2013), 4.2.3.

5. John W. O'Malley, *Trent: What Happened at the Council* (Cambridge, MA: Belknap Press of Harvard University Press, 2013), 99.

6. Congregation for the Clergy, *The Priest and the Third Millennium* (Vatican City: Libreria Editrice Vaticana, 1999), 2.

7. Phillips Brooks, *The Joy of Preaching* (Grand Rapids, MI: Kregel Publications, 1989), 79.

8. Brooks, *Joy of Preaching*, 87.

9. Aristotle, *On Rhetoric*, 1403b.

10. Gregory the Great, *Pastoral Care* (New York: Newman Press, 1978), 2.4.

11. John Eudes Bamberger, *Evagrius Ponticus: The Praktikos, Chapters on Prayer* (Kalamazoo, MI: Cistercian Publications, 1981), 56.

# 4. The Preacher at Prayer

1. Columba Marmion, *Christ—the Ideal of the Priest: Spiritual Conferences* (London: Sands, 1953), 242.

2. *Fulfilled in Your Hearing: The Homily in the Sunday Assembly* (Washington, DC: United States Catholic Conference, 1982), 11, 39.

3. Augustine, *Teaching Christianity*, trans. Edmund Hill (Hyde Park, NY: New City Press, 2013), 4.15.32.

4. Benedict XVI, *Dogma and Preaching: Applying Christian Doctrine to Daily Life*, trans. Michael J. Miller and Matthew J. O'Connell (San Francisco: Ignatius Press, 2011), 103.

5. Benedict XVI, *Dogma and Preaching*, 92.

6. *Code of Canon Law Annotated* (Montréal: Wilson & Lafleur, 2004), 1174 §1.

7. George Guiver, *Company of Voices: Daily Prayer and the People of God* (Norwich, UK: Canterbury, 2001), 39.

8. Clement of Alexandria, *The Stromata*, in *Ante-Nicene Fathers: Volume II. Fathers of the Second Century: Tatian, Theophilus of Antioch, Athenagoras of Athens, Clement of Alexandria* (Edinburgh: T and T Clark, 1994), 7.6–7. Origen, *On Prayer*, in *Origen*, trans. Rowan A. Greer (New York: Paulist Press, 1979), 12.2.

9. Benedict XVI, *Dogma and Preaching*, 15.

10. Peter Ochs, "Morning Prayer as Redemptive Thinking," in *Liturgy, Time, and the Politics of Redemption*, ed. Randi Rashkover and C. C. Pecknold (Grand Rapids, MI: Wm. B. Eerdmans Publishing Co., 2006), 56–57.

11. John Cassian, *Conferences*, in *The Conferences of John Cassian: The Wisdom of the Desert* (Philadelphia: Xlibris, 2002), 10.10.

12. *Fulfilled in Your Hearing*, 36–38.

13. Cf. John Paul II, *Pastores Dabo Vobis* (Washington, DC: United States Catholic Conference, 1992), 26; Pontifical Biblical Commission, *The Interpretation of the Bible in the Church* (Rome: Libreria Editrice Vaticana, 1993), 4.100.2; Francis *Evangelii Gaudium*, 152.

14. For an excellent introduction of the history and development of lectio divina, see Raymond Studzinski, *Reading to Live: The Evolving Practice of Lectio Divina* (Trappist, KY: Cistercian Publications, 2009). Also see Tim Gray, *Praying Scripture for a Change: An Introduction to Lectio Divina* (West Chester, PA: Ascension Press, 2009).

15. Studzinski, *Reading to Live*, 196.

16. Jean Leclercq, *The Love of Learning and the Desire for God: A Study of Monastic Culture* (New York: Fordham University Press, 1974), 14.

17. Studzinski, *Reading to Live*, 118. Leclerq, *Love of Learning and the Desire for God*, 16.

18. *The Interpretation of the Bible in the Church*, IV.A.1.

19. Studzinski, *Reading to Live*, 215.

20. Studzinski, *Reading to Live*, 221.

21. Carol Harrison, *The Art of Listening in the Early Church* (Oxford: Oxford University Press, 2015), 154.

22. Studzinski, *Reading to Live*, 98.

23. John Wortley, *Give Me a Word: The Alphabetical Sayings of the Desert Fathers* (Yonkers, NY: St. Vladimir's Seminary Press, 2014), 243.

24. Thomas Aquinas, *Summa Theologica* (Allen, TX: Christian Classics, 1981), III, q. 40, a. 1, ad. 2.

25. Jean-Pierre Torrell, *Saint Thomas Aquinas*, vol. 1, trans. Robert Royal (Washington, DC: Catholic University of America Press, 2005), 284.

26. Hans Urs von Balthasar, *Prayer* (San Francisco: Ignatius Press, 1986), 155.

27. Balthasar, *Prayer*, 40, 26.

28. Dietrich Bonhoeffer, *The Cost of Discipleship* (New York: Simon and Schuster, 1995), 89.

29. Philip Rousseau, *Pachomius: The Making of a Community in Fourth-Century Egypt* (Berkeley: University of California Press, 1999), 141.

30. Balthasar, *Prayer*, 224.

31. Balthasar, *Prayer*, 9.

32. Ignatius of Loyola, *The Spiritual Exercises of St. Ignatius*, trans. by Louis J. Puhl (Chicago: Loyola Press, 2003), 1.15.

33. Benedict XVI, *Dogma and Preaching*, 101.

34. Josef Pieper, *Happiness and Contemplation* (South Bend, IN: St. Augustine's Press, 1998), 56; cf. *Summa Theologica*, I, q. 27, a. 1.

35. Phillips Brooks, *The Joy of Preaching* (Grand Rapids, MI: Kregel Publications, 1989), 122.

# 5. The Way of Preparation

1. Raymond E. Brown, *The Gospel According to John*, vol. 29 (Garden City, NY: Anchor Bible, 1966), 83.

2. Augustine, *Homilies on the Gospel of John*, in *The Works of Saint Augustine: A Translation for the 21st Century*, vol. 12, trans. Edmund Hill (Hyde Park, NY: New City Press, 2009), 7.17.

3. Thomas Aquinas, *Commentary on the Gospel of John*, trans. Fabian R. Larcher (Lander, WY: Aquinas Institute for the Study of Sacred Doctrine, 2013), C. 1 L. 16 320.

4. Plato, *Gorgias*, trans. Donald J. Zeyl (Indianapolis: Hackett, 1987), 462b–66a.

5. Jaroslav Pelikan, *Christianity and Classical Culture: The Metamorphosis of Natural Theology in the Christian Encounter with Hellenism* (Philadelphia: University of Pennsylvania Press, 2010), 15.

6. Fred B. Craddock, *Preaching* (Nashville: Abingdon Press, 1997), 212.

7. *Fulfilled in Your Hearing: The Homily in the Sunday Assembly* (Washington, DC: United States Catholic Conference, 1982), 29.

8. Phillips Brooks, *The Joy of Preaching* (Grand Rapids, MI: Kregel Publications, 1989), 79.

9. *Fulfilled in Your Hearing*, 39.

10. Walter J. Burghardt, *Preaching: The Art and the Craft* (London: Hodder and Stoughton, 1988), 14.

11. Mervyn A. Warren, *King Came Preaching: The Pulpit Power of Dr. Martin Luther King Jr.* (Downers Grove, IL: InterVarsity Press, 2001), 156.

12. Thomas G. Long, *The Witness of Preaching* (Louisville, KY: Westminster John Knox Press, 2005), 17.

13. Aristotle, *On Rhetoric: A Theory of Civic Discourse*, trans. George A. Kennedy (Oxford University Press, 2007), 1355a-1356a.

14. Brown, *Gospel*, 502.

15. Simone Weil, *Waiting for God* (New York: Harper and Row, 1973), 112.

16. Weil, *Waiting for God*, 112.

17. Romano Guardini, *Letters from Lake Como: Explorations in Technology and the Human Race*, trans. Geoffrey William Bromiley (Grand Rapids, MI: Wm. B. Eerdmans Publishing Co., 1994), 111.

18. Long, *Witness of Preaching*, 97.

19. Paul Ricoeur, *Interpretation Theory: Discourse and the Surplus of Meaning* (Fort Worth: Texas Christian University Press, 1976), 74.

20. Long, *Witness of Preaching*, 97.

21. Henri de Lubac, *Scripture in the Tradition*, trans. Luke O'Neill (New York: Crossroad, 2015), 222.

22. Augustine, *Sermon 265C*, in *Sermons (230–272B) on the Liturgical Seasons*, trans. Edmund Hill (New Rochelle, NY: New City Press, 1994), 1.

23. *The Roman Missal*, 113.

24. Geoffrey Wainwright, *Doxology: The Praise of God in Worship, Doctrine and Life* (New York: Oxford University Press, 1984), 175–77.

25. Aristotle, *On Rhetoric*, 1359b.

26. Gregory the Great, *Pastoral Care* (New York: Newman Press, 1978), 3, prologue.

27. Benedict XVI, *Dogma and Preaching: Applying Christian Doctrine to Daily Life*, trans. Michael J. Miller and Matthew J. O'Connell (San Francisco: Ignatius Press, 2011), 20.

28. Aristotle, *On Rhetoric*, 1355a.

29. *Sesame Street*, episode 1839, produced by Fran Kaufman, November 24, 1983 PBS.

30. Amy Hollingsworth, *The Simple Faith of Mister Rogers: Spiritual Insights from the World's Most Beloved Neighbor* (Nashville: Integrity Publishers, 2005), 138.

31. *Fulfilled in Your Hearing*, 7.

32. Brooks, *Joy of Preaching*, 26.

33. Fred B. Craddock, *Overhearing the Gospel* (Nashville: Abingdon Press, 1988), 43, 50.

34. Augustine, *Teaching Christianity*, trans. Edmund Hill (Hyde Park, NY: New City Press, 2013), 4.28.61.

35. Georg Holzherr, *The Rule of Benedict: An Invitation to the Christian Life*, trans. Mark Thamert (Collegeville, MN: Cistercian Publications, 2016), 86.

36. United States Conference of Catholic Bishops, *Preaching the Mystery of Faith: The Sunday Homily* (Washington, DC: United States Conference of Catholic Bishops, 2013), 33.

37. Georges Bernanos, *The Diary of a Country Priest*, trans. Pamela Morris (New York: Carroll and Graf, 1987), 8.

38. Jonathan Rieder, *Gospel of Freedom: Martin Luther King, Jr.'s Letter from Birmingham Jail and the Struggle That Changed a Nation* (New York: Bloomsbury Press, 2014), 41.

39. Rieder, *Gospel of Freedom*, 181.

40. Rieder, *Gospel of Freedom*, 128.

41. Rieder, *Gospel of Freedom*, 160.

# 6. The Way of Speaking

1. Aristotle, *On Rhetoric: A Theory of Civic Discourse*, trans. George A. Kennedy (New York: Oxford University Press, 2007), 1403a.

2. Thomas G. Long, *The Witness of Preaching* (Louisville, KY: Westminster John Knox Press, 2005), 108.

3. Phillips Brooks, *The Joy of Preaching* (Grand Rapids, MI: Kregel Publications, 1989), 26.

4. Aristotle, *On Rhetoric*, 1403b.

5. Aristotle, *On Rhetoric*, 1403b–1420b.

6. Fred B. Craddock, *Preaching* (Nashville: Abingdon Press, 1997), 190.

7. Ken Untener, *Preaching Better: Practical Suggestions for Homilists* (New York: Paulist Press, 1999), 52.

8. Robert F. Morneau, "Preaching as a Spiritual Exercise," in *A Handbook for Catholic Preaching*, ed. Edward Foley (Collegeville, MN: Liturgical Press, 2016), 10.

9. Untener, *Preaching Better*, 35.

10. Aristotle, *On Rhetoric*, 1416b.

11. William Harmless, *Augustine and the Catechumenate* (Collegeville, MN: Liturgical Press, 2014), 193.

12. Augustine, *Instructing Beginners in Faith*, trans. Raymond Canning (Hyde Park, NY: New City Press, 2006), 7, 11.

13. Michael White and Tom Corcoran, *Rebuilt: The Story of a Catholic Parish* (Notre Dame, IN: Ave Maria Press, 2013), 147.

14. James Mallon, *Divine Renovation: Bringing Your Parish from Maintenance to Mission* (New London, CT: Twenty-Third Publications, 2014), 23.

15. "Our Organization," TED, accessed March 5, 2018, https://www.ted.com/about/our-organization.

16. Augustine, *Instructing Beginners in Faith*, 13, 18.

17. Long, *Witness of Preaching*, 124–34.

18. Long, *Witness of Preaching*, 171.

19. Long, *Witness of Preaching*, 136.

20. Long, *Witness of Preaching*, 108.

21. Fred B. Craddock, *As One Without Authority* (St. Louis: Chalice Press, 2001), 45.

22. Craddock, *As One Without Authority*, 47.

23. *The Roman Missal*, 132.

24. Craddock, *As One Without Authority*, 49.

25. Fred B. Craddock, *Overhearing the Gospel* (Nashville: Abingdon Press, 1988), 137.

26. Aristotle, *On Rhetoric*, 1393a.

27. Cicero, *The Orator*, in *Cicero*, vol. 5, trans. G. L. Hendrickson and Harry Mortimer Hubbell (Cambridge, MA: Harvard University Press, 1971), 18.61.

28. Aristotle, *On Rhetoric*, 1404b–14a.

29. Aristotle, *On Rhetoric*, 1404a.

30. Phillips Brooks, *The Joy of Preaching* (Grand Rapids, MI: Kregel Publications, 1989), 134.

31. Dale Carnegie Training, *Stand and Deliver: How to Become a Masterful Communicator and Public Speaker* (New York: Simon and Schuster, 2011), 1.

32. Plato, *Gorgias*, trans. Donald J. Zeyl (Indianapolis: Hackett, 1987), 462b–66a.

33. Untener, *Preaching Better*, 122.

34. Aristotle, *On Rhetoric*, 1408a.

35. John Henry Newman, "The Crucifixion," in *Parochial and Plain Sermons* (San Francisco: Ignatius Press, 1997), 1500.

36. Augustine, *Instructing Beginners in Faith*, 2, 4.

37. Brooks, *Joy of Preaching*, 134.

38. A. A. Milne, *The House at Pooh Corner* (New York: Puffin/Troll, 1992), 149.

39. Milne, *House at Pooh Corner*, 153.

40. Milne, *House at Pooh Corner*, 160.

41. Milne, *House at Pooh Corner*, 148.

# 7. The Way of Criticism

1. Fred B. Craddock, *Preaching* (Nashville: Abingdon Press, 1997), 65.

2. Cicero, *The Orator*, in *Cicero*, vol. 5, trans. G. L. Hendrickson and Harry Mortimer Hubbell (Cambridge, MA: Harvard University Press, 1971), 21.69; Augustine, *Teaching Christianity*, trans. Edmund Hill (Hyde Park, NY: New City Press, 2013), 4.12.27, 4.15.32.

3. Augustine, *Teaching Christianity*, 4.27.60.

4. Phillips Brooks, *The Joy of Preaching* (Grand Rapids, MI: Kregel Publications, 1989), 146.

5. Augustine, *City of God: Against the Pagans*, trans. Henry Bettenson (Middlesex, UK: Penguin, 1984), 14.28.

6. Augustine, *Instructing Beginners in Faith*, trans. Raymond Canning (Hyde Park, NY: New City Press, 2006), 2, 3.

7. *Fulfilled in Your Hearing: The Homily in the Sunday Assembly* (Washington, DC: United States Catholic Conference, 1982), 15.

8. Yves Congar, *Lay People in the Church: A Study for a Theology of Laity* (London: G. Chapman, 1985), 294.

9. Ken Untener, *Preaching Better: Practical Suggestions for Homilists* (New York: Paulist Press, 1999), 99.

10. Augustine, *Instructing Beginners in Faith*, 10, 14.

11. Carol Harrison, *The Art of Listening in the Early Church* (Oxford: Oxford University Press, 2015), 144.

12. Untener, *Preaching Better*, 99.

13. Untener, *Preaching Better*, 2–4.

14. Untener, *Preaching Better*, 2–4.

15. Craddock, *Preaching*, 22.

16. *General Instruction of the Roman Missal* (Washington, DC: United States Conference of Catholic Bishops, 2003), 66; cf. United States

Conference of Catholic Bishops, *Preaching the Mystery of Faith* (Washington, DC: United States Conference of Catholic Bishops, 2013),17.

17. James Mallon, *Divine Renovation: Bringing Your Parish from Maintenance to Mission* (New London, CT: Twenty-Third Publications, 2014), 54.

18. *The Martyr Act of Lyons and Vienne*, in *The Acts of the Christian Martyrs*, trans. Herbert Musurillo (Oxford: Oxford University Press, 2000), 1.9–10.

19. Joshua J. Whitfield, *Pilgrim Holiness: Martyrdom as Descriptive Witness* (Eugene, OR: Cascade Books, 2009), 46.

20. Craddock, *Preaching*, 188.

21. David J. Garrow, *Bearing the Cross: Martin Luther King, Jr., and the Southern Christian Leadership Conference* (New York: Vintage Books, 1988), 58.

22. Dietrich Bonhoeffer, *The Cost of Discipleship* (New York: Simon and Schuster, 1995), 218.

23. Augustine, *Sermons (230–272B) on the Liturgical Seasons*, vol. 7, trans. Edmund Hill (New Rochelle, NY: New City Press, 1994), 232.8.

# 8. The Pentecost of Preaching

1. Phillips Brooks, *The Joy of Preaching* (Grand Rapids, MI: Kregel Publications, 1989), 25.

2. Benedict XVI, *Dogma and Preaching: Applying Christian Doctrine to Daily Life*, trans. Michael J. Miller and Matthew J. O'Connell (San Francisco: Ignatius Press, 2011), 40.

3. Hans Urs von Balthasar, *Prayer* (San Francisco: Ignatius Press, 1986), 81.

4. *Fulfilled in Your Hearing: The Homily in the Sunday Assembly* (Washington, DC: United States Catholic Conference, 1982), 42.

5. Augustine, *Teaching Christianity*, trans. Edmund Hill (Hyde Park, NY: New City Press, 2013), 4.15.32.

6. United States Conference of Catholic Bishops, *Preaching the Mystery of Faith: The Sunday Homily* (Washington, DC: United States Conference of Catholic Bishops, 2013), 19.

7. Paul Türks, *Philip Neri: The Fire of Joy* (Edinburgh: T and T Clark, 1995), 17.

8. Türks, *Philip Neri*, 113.

9. Türks, *Philip Neri*, 44.

10. Brooks, *Joy of Preaching*, 47.

11. William Shakespeare, *Henry V* (New York: Simon & Schuster, 2009), Prologue, 1–2.

# Epilogue: The Way of the Listener

1. John C. Cavadini, "Simplifying Augustine," in *Educating People of Faith: Exploring the History of Jewish and Christian Communities*, ed. John Van Engen (Grand Rapids, MI: Wm. B. Eerdmans Publishing Co., 2004), 74, 77.

2. *The Roman Missal*, 144.

3. Augustine, *Teaching Christianity*, trans. Edmund Hill (Hyde Park, NY: New City Press, 2013), 4.13.29.

4. Plutarch, *Moralia*, vol. 1, trans. Frank Cole Babbitt (Cambridge, MA: Harvard University Press, 1986), 3.

5. John Chrysostom, *Six Books on the Priesthood*, trans. Graham Neville (Yonkers, NY: St. Vladimir's Seminary Press, 1996), 2.4.

6. Óscar A. Romero, *The Violence of Love*, trans. James R. Brockman (Maryknoll, NY: Orbis Books, 2010), 48.

7. Wendell Berry, *Jayber Crow* (Washington, DC: Counterpoint, 2000), 162.

8. H. van der Looy, *Rule for a New Brother* (London: Darton, Longman and Todd, 1986), 36.

9. Thomas S. Kidd, *The Great Awakening* (New Haven, CT: Yale University Press, 2007), 62.

10. Aristotle, *On Rhetoric: A Theory of Civic Discourse*, trans. George A. Kennedy (New York: Oxford University Press, 2007), 1416b.

11. Augustine, *Teaching Christianity*, 4.24.53.

12. Henri Ghéon, *The Secret of the Curé d'Ars*, trans. F. J. Sheed (London: Sheed and Ward, 1948), 44.

13. Simone Weil, *The Need for Roots: Prelude to a Declaration of Duties towards Mankind*, trans. Arthur Wills (London: Routledge, 2010), 14.

14. Thomas Aquinas, *Summa Theologica* (Allen, TX: Christian Classics, 1981), II-II, q. 4, a. 3.

15. Aelred of Rievaulx, *Spiritual Friendship*, trans. Mary Eugenia Laker (Kalamazoo, MI: Cistercian Publications, 1977), 1.1.

16. Raymond Studzinski, *Reading to Live: The Evolving Practice of Lectio Divina* (Trappist, KY: Cistercian Publications, 2009), 130.

17. Geoffrey Wainwright, *Doxology: The Praise of God in Worship, Doctrine and Life* (New York: Oxford University Press, 1984), 175–77.